Property Development

The Secrets to Becoming a Property Developer, From Scratch, Using None of Your Own Money

By Lloyd Girardi

Stop dreaming of the life you'd love and start living the life that you dream.

Lloyd Girardi

Table of Contents

Introduction

Thank you for purchasing this book. I wrote it to help those interested to better understand and enter the property development market.

Property development, even if begun as more of a hobby or side interest, is a business. So you need to treat it like a business.

It is a big step up from traditional property investing. If you are uncertain as to whether you have what it takes to do property development, then my advice is: Don't start. At least not until you read this book, cover to cover.

Property development is risky. I am not trying to convince you otherwise. You need to have the belief and desire to want to get into property development in order for it to be rewarding – rewarding in both a monetary and a personal sense. It is not for everyone.

Property developments are for those who like a challenge. You will have days where you will face some tough decisions – all developers do. Timescales will likely slip. But with every downside, there is an upside.

How well you plan, prepare, and cope with the challenges is what will see you succeed. In these chapters, I guide you through some of the property deals that I and my business partner, Andi Cooke, have completed, won, and lost. Here, I share tips and techniques we have learned and successfully used over the past few years.

I also share some of our highs and, more importantly, lows, along with our best and honest advice to help motivate the first-timer to take the scariest step – that very first step – and get into developments. If you are a first-timer, I hope you find yourself inspired. What is important is to be open minded reading this book and then ask yourself afterwards: Is this for me?

If you have been doing property developments for a while, this book may well shed light on some things you may not know or have yet to encounter, and perhaps might do differently after having read about it. We have trained experienced developers in the past, and they have implemented some of the techniques we use, and their business has benefited as a result. You don't know what you don't know.

Andi and I created our development business from scratch, and we have managed to build it using none of our own money. You can too. As you will discover in this book, I started with no money at all, no development experience, and an additional full-time job.

Others may insist this can't be done, that you can't start a property development business using none of your own money. But ask yourself this: Don't most companies start with nothing? Businesses raise capital by soliciting investors – venture capitalists, banks, even family and friends – and pay them back from future profits and grow from there. We have implemented a business mind-set to property development.

Back when I first contemplated entering the business, I would have been sceptical if someone told me I could create a property development business using none of my own money. But having gone through the process, from those first baby steps to where we are now, I can assure you that it most certainly is possible. We are living proof. You can use none of your own money and reap the rewards that property developing can bring. At this present moment, while writing this book, our property portfolio stands at 161 units. That might sound impressive to you, it might not, but this has been achieved in just four years. From a standing start, without any of our own money, through relationships and joint ventures. We have made many friends along the way and helped as many people out as we can. We've been told we share too much sometimes, but we don't care. We needed as much help when we started, so we want to give at least as much back.

One thing is for sure, and this is one of the secrets: It takes time, it takes patience, it takes dedication, and it takes effort. This isn't a Get Rich Quick strategy. It's a Make Money by Being Prepared to Work for It strategy. The biggest challenge? To get started. This book shows you how. It illustrates, step by step, how we have done it, and how you can do it. To make it even easier for you, we have listed all of our team members' contact information throughout and at the end of the book, because they're terrific, and worth every penny and then some.

I discuss how to find property development deals, give you examples of how to fund them, and how, with just some willingness from you, to become a property developer.

Over the years, I have worked on my own personal development and believe that with the right mind-set, attitude, determination, persistence, and desire, you can achieve anything you like.

Ask yourself: Who is the best in doing what you want to achieve? Who is at the top of their game?

Whoever it might be, model them. Look into them, and not up to them. Find out why they are great and model them. That is how to get what you want. What makes them successful? They're not fundamentally different to you or me. Everyone has the same amount of time in a day. Not one person on the planet has an extra second in a day more than anyone else.

What makes them different is discipline. They are undoubtedly disciplined and driven. If you have a reason, and the reason is big enough, nothing can get in your way.

I want to inspire you to strive for your goals, no matter what those goals are. Even if it isn't property development you want, you can apply these principles towards whatever you want to achieve most.

Go for it! You are the only one who can stand in your way.

Chapter 1 The Auction

It was a chilly February morning. The room was set with about 150 standard hotel-style conference chairs, upholstered in red, set in neat rows on either side of a centre aisle. They were the kind that if I put my hand underneath, I'd expect to find wads of hardened Wrigley's chewing gum.

I looked around, nervously. The room seemed very large to me, despite the number of people milling about. I studied their faces. Everyone else seemed calm, relaxed. Were we the only ones who had no idea what we were doing, or what to expect? As more people made their way inside, we found two seats on the left-hand side, about halfway back, with about five rows in front of us.

I took a deep breath. What the fuck am I doing? Am I doing the right thing? Sitting down, I studied the others there, trying to gauge what they did. Who might be there to bid on the property my partner Andi and I were interested in?

Security cameras dotted the room, including one just to the left of me, above the fire exit. It seemed to be pointing directly at me, with laser-like focus. Why all these cameras? What are they for? Am I being watched? My mind was racing a mile a minute. I took another deep breath, trying to ignore how shaky I felt. Andi, I assumed, must be feeling the same anxiety. I glanced at him. He, too, was looking about, studying the other potential bidders.

The auctioneer stepped forward, to the front of the room, and stood on a raised platform, asking people to take their seats and quieten down, exuding an air of calm authority. He recognised a few friendly faces, perhaps regulars to the auction, and nodded to the chairs with a gentle smile. Everyone took their seats and conversation ceased. Only the noise of the heaters could be heard.

As he introduced himself, the auctioneer paused and momentarily locked eyes with me. I froze, convinced that if I blinked, shuffled, or so much as twitched, I would be perceived as having bid on something, and the auction hadn't even commenced yet. This was a huge step for me, and something that was completely out of my comfort zone. It felt bizarre. I had never done this kind of thing before.

Andi and I were interested in a plot of land in our local town, Northampton, that was being auctioned, and had spent the past three weeks researching the area and the property market. We researched how much houses were selling for in the area and discussed it exhaustively. We visualised how it would look once we had finished building it. We scribbled numerous different outcomes on paper, spanning best, most likely, and worst-case scenarios, and I created a spreadsheet to illustrate our workings out. It was all guesswork at the time. This was new to both of us.

But it was something we knew we both wanted.

The site was twenty-two former council lock-up garages set on 0.3 acres and tucked in between two rows of Victorian terraced houses to the right and in front, and a block of flats to the rear and left. A private driveway led from St James Park Road.

I stood in the middle of the site and looked around. There was litter everywhere. The wind was gusting, lifting bits and pieces to create a tornado of crap and discarding them in every corner. Some of the garages were locked, some gaped open, the doors missing, and others were boarded up.

I walked about and casually looked inside the open garages, which were filled with Tennent's Super beer cans and various bits of rubbish. What an eyesore, I thought.

I glanced around at the Victorian houses that lined one corner of the site. All had their rear gardens facing this virtual tip, with access gates set inside the six-foot brick wall that divided the properties, providing those residents with access.

I shivered slightly and caught my partner's eye with a questioning look. It was freezing on this late January morning of 2014. Andi and I were silent as we soaked it all in, knowing this was crazy. We had been tossing around the idea of building some houses on this spot. We were not developers. This was new to both Andi and me.

But we also knew the time was right.

We would buy it. We would attend the auction.

So now, here we were, at the auction, ready to buy. Well, kind of. Knowing how important it was, we had established a figure that we had agreed we were not prepared to go past. That figure was £150,000.

We had hoped we would be given the opportunity to watch a few lots be auctioned off first, before our own target property came up for bid, just to see how things were done, but as luck would have it, our site was lot number 1. The guide price was shown as £100,000–125,000.

'I start the bidding at eighty thousand', the auctioneer announced. No one moved, including us. After a very long moment, a middle-aged gentleman to our right, a few rows ahead of us, raised his hand. Another hand appeared four rows behind him. The bidding had started.

'Ninety, ninety-five, one hundred thousand, one hundred and

five thousand…' Andi and I turned our heads slightly to watch the room, afraid to move, as the bidding continued.

I swallowed hard. With every hand, the price increased by another five thousand. I was sure that if I looked down, I would be able to see my pounding heart as it tried to escape my chest. My hands were shaking, my palms clammy.

When the bidding reached £135,000, I nodded to Andi. Before the auction had begun, I had said to him, 'You're doing the bidding, okay? I'm shitting myself, and I'm afraid to move a muscle.'

Andi calmly raised his hand. We were quickly outbid by what looked like a couple of builders standing at the back of the room. By this time the auctioneer had reduced the incremental increases to £2,000.

'One hundred and thirty-nine thousand', the auctioneer said, in response to Andi's signal.

I risked a quick look around. The bids were slowing down, the bidders dropping out, one by one. Unfortunately, my heart was doing the opposite, beating a brisk staccato. It was down to just the builders and us now, it looked like.

'One hundred and forty-one thousand', the taller of the builders shouted. The eyes of the auctioneer flicked from him to us.

'Do I have one hundred and forty-three thousand?' the auctioneer asked. Andi nodded.

The auctioneer's gaze returned to the builders.

'One hundred and forty-five thousand?' he asked. I felt my jaw drop when they shook their heads.

Holy shit! No one else was bidding. We were winning! Buying twenty-two garages for £143,000!

I felt a thrill run through me, followed by a chill. We didn't exactly have £143,000, or any idea yet how to get it. We were complete novices, having never developed before, and with just two buy-to-let properties between us. With all of the research and work we had done over the past three weeks, that was the only thing we hadn't yet nailed down. So, you might be thinking it was pretty stupid sitting in an auction, bidding on something we had no money for and no real idea of how to get the money for it.

'Going once, at one hundred and forty-three thousand pounds...'

There was silence. My raspy breath thundered in my ears.

'Going twice at one hundred and forty-three thousand pounds...'

Again, nothing. The auctioneer slowly raised his hammer in preparation to strike and finalise the sale. With the crack of the hammer against the desk, the plot of land would be legally ours. It looked as though we had won the lot. It looked as though we were just about to purchase a plot of land in the middle of Northampton that we had spent weeks looking into. This is it, we were about to win.

But wait...

A black biro slowly rose, barely high enough to see, from a chair in front of us.

'One hundred and forty-five thousand', offered the little old lady. My jaw dropped. This wobbling black biro had just outbid us! Just as we were about the win the lot. Gutted, but not to be outdone, we raised the bid to £147,000. The biro appeared again, the frail-looking hand shaking slightly.

I glanced at Andi, our maximum bid of £150,000 looming. We bid again, this time at £149,000.

Again, the biro was lifted, raising the bid now just over our maximum, to £151,000. We were so close. Andi and I looked at each other and nodded. He bid £153,000. Disheartened, I watched her response: £155,000.

Up and up we crawled, until the lady bid £163,000. That was it. We knew we had to stop. Distraught, we heard the auctioneer solicit again, to be met with silence.

'Sold!' he called.

We'd lost. We'd been so close, thinking we had it at £143,000. The lady stood up and walked to the back of the room to fill out the legal paperwork. What did she want with twenty-two lock-up garages, I wondered? We sat there, numb, as the next three auction lots were bid on, one by one.

A tap on Andi's shoulder caused him to turn. It was the little old lady. In halting English, as the auction continued around us, she asked him loud enough for others to hear whether he had been the one who had bid against her.

Andi got to his feet and followed her and a member of the auction staff out of the room, unsure what was happening. Had she made a mistake? Why would she have asked Andi if he had been the one bidding against her? We would soon find out.

She didn't want the garages. She had made a mistake. She thought she was bidding on a hairdressers on the Wellingborough Road, also in Northampton. (Which, by the way, was lot number 3 and had just sold to someone else for £135,000, £27,000 less than what she had bid for the garages.) But at auction, she is legally tied into that lot from the moment that the slam of the hammer is forced into the wooden block.

The auctioneers rang the owner of the garages, who had left the room the instant he had sold his plot and was probably in the pub by now, celebrating his sale. After the auctioneer explained the situation, he said he would be happy to sell it to us instead.

Whilst pleased, we were also angered that, thanks to her mistake, she had marched the price up from our nearly winning bid of £143,000 by another £20,000.

As it turned out, the reserve was £157,000. We agreed to purchase the site for the £157,000, with the lady agreeing to pay us £1,000 to basically get her out of the shit.

To date, we still haven't received that £1,000 from her. Hmm... I wonder if she'll ever read this book? I hope so, just so we can thank her.

So, on the 19th February 2014, we purchased our first ever development deal, which kicked off our property development business. (We'll talk about how we successfully raised the funds to close the purchase in chapter 3.)

So, can you see why I say that anyone with willingness can do this? We are no-one special. We hadn't had years and years of experience, we didn't start with bags and bags of money, and I didn't even have all that much time to concentrate on developments. But what we did do, what set us apart, was to start.

Zig Ziglar famously said, 'You don't have to be great to start, but you have to start to be great.' It's true. You can't achieve something if you never start. You can't think of an idea or a business and expect it to form itself. You have to start it.

When we started, we were far from perfect, and we're not ashamed to admit it. In fact, we like to be honest; we will only tell you the truth, because that's the best way to show you that anything is possible if you want something enough.

Before we continue, maybe sharing a little of my history, what shaped the person I am today, might help you understand my mind-set better.

If you believe in yourself positively enough, only physical positivity can exude.

Secret Tip #1: Go for it. Don't be afraid of what might happen; but think about what might not. If you want something, go for it. We only have one life. Make the most of it. Don't let others stop your vision. Create your own future and only regret not starting.

Chapter 2 A Bit About Me

From a very early age I always wanted my own business. I can't remember how old, or why, and I didn't even know what business. I just liked the idea of being the one to come up with the ideas. As a boy I was always creating games. I would take a game and adapt the rules to make it more interesting.

I was born in Northampton in July, 1986. My mum, Julie, and my dad, Simon, were originally from Skegness, and my dad's job had moved them to Northampton three years earlier. We lived on the first street out of the Collingtree Park Golf Club. Collingtree Park is quite an expensive area of Northampton so I used to say I lived there even though I was just outside of it.

My brother Richard and I shared a room. Whilst polar opposites in character, we had a shared love for building things with Lego, K-Nex and Meccano.

My brother was exacting. When playing with Lego, he would organise all the pieces by colour, size, and shape first, and then start building. Not me. I would tip up the box, ignoring the instructions, and rustle my way through the pile to find the piece I wanted.

I was into sports, where my brother was more into music, maths, and photography. I tried the guitar as a child but found I didn't have the patience to learn. As with most things I started, I quickly lost interest. Whatever sport was on the TV at the time I was playing in the street. In summer, I'd be out playing tennis in the road. When the cricket was on, I'd be outside using the lamppost as stumps and the curbs as my crease. When the winter Olympics were on, I'd be on my roller skates at the top of the street, imagining I was on the Super-G or downhill slalom.

My mum and dad split up when I was about seven, which was hard for many years, mostly because of the tension between my parents. I don't like seeing people upset. I think my brother was more distressed by it than I was, which I put down to me being quite a positive person. I have always been very optimistic, maybe too optimistic at times, but I always try to see the best in any situation, good or bad. I believe that everything has a solution; it just takes a bit of working out to achieve it. I love problem solving.

My mum took care of my brother and me for years on her own. She was amazing. She was the branch manager of the building society Bristol & West, which has since become part of the Bank of Ireland.

I still remember the layout of the Northampton branch. The welcome desk at the front was on the left as you walked in. I used to come in every day after school and eat all of the mint imperials, whilst my mum carried on working. When I was about eight, I remember seeing the safe and getting excited about what was inside. I liked the idea of money. I used to sit upstairs in the staff room drawing on the flip chart – well, the bottom half, as I couldn't reach the top unless I stood on a chair. (That's probably still true today.)

I understood how banks worked but not what a mortgage was at that age. Even whilst playing Monopoly I didn't understand them.

As a child I was creative, always looking to change the rules and make games more interesting. Although I wouldn't call it being entrepreneurial from a young age, I guess there was something in me that always wanted to start something new, and probably explains my desire to start my own business one day.

My mum met my stepdad, Jason, in 1993. He was young at

the time. He also had hair back then. (He'll read this). They got married when I was thirteen, and that's when I started my first business. It lasted about twenty minutes, but it was my first taste of earning money. I had pocket money, but that also lasted about twenty minutes as I'd spend it straight away. I definitely didn't have an investment mind-set back then. Does any kid?

My first business was a spur of the moment thing, kicked off during the wedding of my mum and stepdad. The classic wedding songs were being spun by the DJ: 'Come on, Eileen', 'You Spin Me Right Round' – you know the ones. And, at thirteen, I fancied myself a bit of a dancer. It was more of a wiggle than a dance, but I thought I was good. As it turned out, one of my stepdad's relatives thought I was good too. She gave me 50p for dancing. I had never been paid to dance before. So, I decided to go round to each table and ask them if they would like me to dance. They'd laugh and say, 'Sure!' They had to pay me, I explained. This was the first time I had ever asked for money.

Business was booming for fifteen or twenty minutes. Not having to invest anything myself except time and effort, every penny I earned was profit, and I'd managed to earn about £8.20. I loved it! I think most of my customers did too.

It came to a screeching halt when Mum found out, told me I couldn't dance and take money off people, and demanded I return all of it back to my customers. I was devastated. I sadly refunded the aunties, uncles, and family friends their money and stropped for the rest of the night. But I found I enjoyed making money and making people happy. Looking back, however, I can see my mum's point.

I didn't have many other business ideas for a while.

I went through school enjoying mainly the more creative subjects. I did PE, Photography Technology, Business Studies, Art, Design

Technology, Psychology, Geography, and so on, but I still didn't know what I wanted to do after I got out of school. Most of my friends knew what they wanted to do, or which university they wanted to study at. The only thing I was sure on was that I didn't want to go to university. All of my family and friends were talking to me about going to university and what was I going to study.

I hated the idea of studying a further three years. I was done with education and wanted to travel for a while, although I didn't tell anyone that. I have a thing about flags and wanting to travel to every country in the world.

The deadline came and went to fill in the UCAS forms for university. I didn't fill one in, despite my family thinking I had. Nervous, I eventually confessed to Mum my desire to travel instead of attending university, and to my surprise, she was 100% supportive, and helped me decide where and when. (Maybe she was trying to get rid of me.) I chose New Zealand, as I wanted to do a ski season, and Europe was too close. I wanted to really explore the world. I was going to travel there in 2005. It was also where the British and Irish Lions were touring that year.

In 2004, despite failing the theory test three times, I aced my practical driving test. (I've always preferred practical over theory.) My first car was a silver P reg Ford Fiesta. It was a great first car. I was into the Fast and Furious films and became obsessed with making my car look like one of those cars. The only problems were that I had no money saved and only a 1.2-litre engine. I duct-taped an air filter on instead of using jubilee clips. I was working at the time as a waiter, so all of my earnings were spent on my car and all of my tips on alcohol. My best friend Jason worked with me at Frankie and Bennies and we frequently went out after our shifts finished at 11 p.m. and spent all of our tips. Now, however, I had to save for my trip to New Zealand. Saving wasn't one of my strong points – I preferred to enjoy life. But I had a target of £5,000 to save before I left the following month, January 2005, for New Zealand.

I decided to sell my car, which gave me around £3,000, a miracle considering I had butchered it in my quest for a Fast and Furious motor. Next, I set up a private New Year's Eve taxi service for family friends in the village that I lived In, using my stepdad's car. I created some flyers and posted them through every door a week before to see if I could get some business. It said something like Need a taxi on New Year's Eve? Anywhere, anytime. Help me get to New Zealand.

I got a very good response and booked up very quickly. Here I was, eighteen and legally allowed to go out for New Year's Eve for the first time, and I decided to stay sober and earn some money instead. It proved a smart decision as I earned about £700 that night, including a few airport runs earlier in the day, which was a good money maker. My stepdad generously contributed the cost of my fuel as well as his car to help me raise the money.

It was now January 2005. I packed my bags and went off on my own, but in an organised group. There were about twenty of us in total. I made friends with this guy John, from Newcastle. We both wanted to get to Queenstown, New Zealand, so we decided to buy a camper van. What we bought was a Toyota Lite-Ace and threw a mattress in the back to save money on accommodation. We headed south from Auckland towards Queenstown to find work. We travelled all around the North Island and most of the South Island for a couple of weeks first. Just past Mount Cook, the head gasket blew and we had to ditch the van with a local mechanic a few miles from Queenstown.

Eventually, we made it to Queenstown. Two weeks into the trip, not surprisingly, I had managed to spend most of the money that was supposed to last me for the duration. I found a job in the produce department of Fresh Choice, a local supermarket. After about three weeks, I suggested to the produce manager and owner of the supermarket chain that their layout looked all wrong to me. Again, I wanted to change the rules of the game to make it better.

Before, when you walked into the supermarket, you came straight into the produce section. The fruit and veg were set out like a library where, rather than row after row of shelves and books, it featured refrigerated units with fruit and veg. I asked if I could change the layout overnight so that when the customers came into the store, they had to walk through the produce like a maze, past every fruit and veg. Pretty much overnight, sales increased, which the owner and store manager were over the moon about.

Before I left for New Zealand, my dad had given me a travel journal with a message inside to log my travels and diarise what I did. True to form, I filled it in faithfully for about the first two weeks before getting bored. Instead, it became my business ideas and doodle pad.

One of the business ideas I came up with during my travels was a juice bar, serving fresh, healthy smoothies and shakes every day. (This was before they became so popular.)

Another was the Beer Police, a business that would deliver alcohol, snacks, and mixers to your door. Imagine running out of alcohol at a party. Never fear! The Beer Police are here!

Yeah, I can see why I didn't pursue that one. I still have the journal today though, as it brings back great memories of my travels.

I travelled for thirteen months across New Zealand, Australia, and Fiji and loved every minute of it. The experience travelling on my own helped me get out of my shell a little, as I had been quite a shy kid.

On my return to the UK, despite numerous business ideas, I doubted myself, and life got in the way of my dreams of starting a business. I didn't have a business idea I was motivated enough to pursue, so I got a job instead.

After a short stint at Frankie & Bennies again, I started working for George Wimpey Homes (now Taylor Wimpey Homes, after the merge with Taylor Woodrow). I was a sales executive in the show homes, selling new-build houses. I really enjoyed that job. Most of the time I was on my own, looking after the show homes and sales centres. I loved meeting new people and helping them choose the specs for their new home. It taught me what's important in new-build properties and what comprised a good layout and design in show homes, which comes in handy these days.

I learnt a lot about how the new-build industry works and was trained to sell houses. It was a skill, as buyers were making a life choice, not generally an impulse buy. There were a couple of investors whom I mistakenly thought were impulse buying, as I was unaware that investors, who were cash buyers, purchased houses. I just thought these individuals were simply loaded and had a lot of spare money. I know now that you can buy property using other people's money.

After a year or so, I joined an independent financial mortgage broker in Northampton, where I was responsible for qualifying potential house buyers for mortgages and booking the mortgage advisors' appointments. We were the recommended mortgage broker for a lot of the big builders. I was looking after sites from Barratts, Taylor Wimpey, Bloor Homes, Persimmon, David

Wilson, and Charles Church at the time. It was competitive, which I enjoyed, as I love to hit targets. I'm a very competitive person. I always wanted to be the one at the top of the leader board. That hasn't changed today. If you're going to take part in a competitive activity, why wouldn't you want to be the best? Why wouldn't you want to test yourself and see if you can be top of the leader board?

The company was taken over by the Connells Group in early 2007, and I was made redundant just before the crash, as it happens. Good timing really, looking back.

I was twenty-one. Still not focusing on starting my own business, I joined the sales team of a lighting company in Northampton. The owner spoke to me about the potential to buy the business in a few years, just like he had done from the previous owner. This sparked my interest straight away. With thoughts of a business of my own, I helped the company design their new catalogue whilst being part of the sales team.

After a few years, however, I decided it wasn't the business I wanted to run, so I started looking for other options. One of my customers approached me to come and work for them selling LED lighting, which was fast becoming popular in 2010, and so I did. The company were one of the first to sell bespoke LED ribbons in the UK, so sales were good as we were niche at the time. The owner, two colleagues and I grew the business to sell LED lighting to electrical wholesalers around the UK. My role was external sales. I loved it, as I got to meet and interact with new people, building business relationships. That is something I still love. I love meeting new people and, more importantly, I love helping them out.

Still, my dream of starting my own business was becoming more and more distant. I had worked hard the past eight years but was limited in what I could earn. I wondered whether my dream would remain just that – a dream.

In February 2012, I was in London for the day, visiting some existing wholesale customers and looking to acquire some new ones. It was one of those days where the minutes lasted hours, when you look at the clock and it says 10:04 and, what feels like half an hour later you look again, only to find that a mere three minutes have passed and it's now 10:07.

As night began to fall, I crept up the M11, the traffic moving as swiftly as the preceding hours. My mobile rang. It was my step-mum.

'We've got the results back from your dad's biopsy' were her words to me. 'Can you pop in on your way home?' At this point, the only sound was that of the rain, lashing down onto my front windscreen, and the wipers working hard to clear my vision. Thoughts were chaotically running around in my head and the realisation of what was happening to my dad was all I could think about.

My dad had been suffering dizzy spells for the past few months, and even had a couple of falls. Tests had revealed a mass in his brain.

When I arrived at my dad's house, I knew the news wasn't good.

'Your dad has been diagnosed with a malignant brain tumour and has maybe eight months to live.'

My dad was just 52 at the time. Eight months would take him up to his 53rd birthday in October. We were devastated.

For the next few months, Dad underwent treatment, including chemotherapy, making various trips to Oxford Hospital for tests.

My dad, who had worked for the piano company Yamaha for over 25 years, had been keen for me to learn the guitar as a boy. While I shared his love for music, if you recall, my attempt at the guitar didn't go so well, at least not back then. But when I returned from New Zealand, I taught myself how to play the guitar, and after my dad's diagnosis, I wrote a song, 'Always Believe', to inspire my dad to think positively about his health. I am a strong believer in positivity. If you think positively, then only positive things can happen. I recorded the song and played it for him.

Despite his initial diagnosis of just eight months to live, my dad soldiered on past his October 2012 birthday, and in 2013, there were signs of improvement. The tumour was shrinking. Things were looking good.

My dad had always been a Leicester City football fan. I had the opportunity to play football at the King Power stadium in May 2012, and he watched me play. I scored twice, one admittedly a deflection off my ass from a corner – but they all count – and the other was a blinder, that is, until it was ruled out, outrageously, for offside. (I have video evidence to prove it was outrageous).

My grandad loved the game too. A former player for Sheffield United, he had a choice of becoming a professional footballer or a PE teacher. Back then, PE paid more. During a school football game, one of my grandad's pupils, the team's goalkeeper, wanted to play in midfield. My grandad said to him, 'If you want to play in my team, you will play in goal'. That pupil was Ray Clemence, who would be scouted there by Scunthorpe United, which signed him professionally. Sadly, my grandad was later diagnosed with Alzheimer's, which changed him from the caring, loving, and supportive gentleman that everyone loved. It was heart-breaking to witness. I still loved him. He was an idol to me.

So, football was a big part of my childhood. My dad was assistant manager for my Saturday league team, and back in 1997 I was invited to have trials for Northampton Town, but I didn't make the final cut. I was asked to return next year, but I never did.

My little brother, Scott, however, recently entered a competition with over 20,000 applicants to join the YouTube football team Hashtag United. He won and joined the team in 2017.

I am super proud of him, and jealous, as he played at Wembley in the Wembley Cup, alongside former legends of the game as teammates: Robbie Fowler, Robbie Savage, and William Gallas, playing against David James, Emile Heskey, and Steven Gerrard. Not only that but Scott was eventually chosen the man of the match. I'd like to think I taught him everything he knows. He will be a superstar in the future. You heard it here first.

Despite my dad soldiering on way past his initial diagnosis and the tumour showed signs of decreasing at times, he started to deteriorate in August 2013. While I was on holiday in Italy, I received a call from my step-mum to say that my dad had been taken to Northampton General Hospital after a fall at home. As soon as I arrived home, I went to see him in hospital. For weeks I was there by his bed, despite not having as close relationship with my dad, after my mum and dad split up. He was my dad, after all.

During the time in hospital with him, my mind was thinking of all sorts of things. I questioned myself as to why I had never started the business that I had always wanted. Why does it take life-changing moments like this to spur us to reflect on what we have missed out on? Why, when faced with a close family member in hospital, should it take moments like this to question your own future?

On Monday, the 4th November 2013, the phone rang at 7:35

a.m. I remember the time because I was just about to leave the house to go to work. It was the hospice, where my dad had been for the past few weeks, asking me to come. I bolted out the door.

I arrived shortly after 8:10. My step-mum, Helen, my younger sister Elise, and my brother Scott had arrived moments before.

None of us reached him in time. In tears, heartbroken, I was determined to make a change. It was that very day I said to myself: I am going to live my dream. I am going to make my dad proud and start my own business. I am going to make my family proud.

In the weeks that followed, I was determined to start my business. I questioned business owners that I knew as to how they had got started. I needed to find out from people who had done it before and had done it successfully. I believe that is the best way to learn.

It was during those weeks following the passing of my dad that my grandad was also in and out of hospital. It was testing times for me. I had to remain strong. I was determined to make my family proud. On the 30th December 2013, my grandad passed away. If ever I had a reason to follow my dreams, this had just been cemented 57 days after my dad's death.

Andi is my wife's cousin. He and I have known each other since I started dating my wife, Lydia. We saw each other at the occasional family party, but we never truly knew much about each other, professionally. I knew Andi had his own business, Redbox Developments, because it was written on the side of his van, but I had no idea what Red Box did. Likewise, Andi knew I worked for a lighting company, but that was all he knew. We typically only met during family parties. You know how family parties go. Each year you turn up, see the same faces, and ask the same questions: How are you? How's work? But this time it was different, as I quizzed Andi about how he had started his business.

Andi's property journey started in about 2004, when his uncle, an architect, wanted to move back to Northamptonshire. He and his wife had separated, and after renting a flat on his own in a town that never really felt like home, he decided that when he retired at 67 he wanted to move back to Higham Ferrers, where his relatives still lived. Unfortunately, the separation had proved costly, and apart from a good pension, he didn't have sufficient funds to buy a house.

Andi was working for an audio-visual company in Northampton, and his wife Debbie was a psychiatric nurse. Andi was intrigued by the property world, but had no idea how to get involved, or whether it was even viable for people with 'normal' jobs, on an average wage. It was while visiting his uncle that he thought maybe he could secure the mortgage and buy the house for his uncle to rent, enough to offset the mortgage and bills. It would be his uncle's home for as long as he wanted it, but Andi would own it.

In April 2007, shortly after his second son was born and Debbie was still on maternity leave, Andi abruptly quit his job. He had had enough and wanted something different. It wasn't an easy decision, but he knew it was time to start a business, something he had always wanted to do. However, like me, he wasn't quite sure what it was he wanted to do. And having sunk most of his savings into the down payment on his uncle's house, he needed to earn money straight away to keep paying the bills.

Andi took on any job that he could find, jobs that he could do straight away. He wasn't a qualified carpenter, but he had been working with wood for the past ten years in different roles. He began designing and building stages and sets. He also worked for a library-fitting company, and fitted kitchens, bathrooms, and tiled floors for a while. He basically did anything he could get his hands on.

That marked the birth of Redbox Developments. Andi wanted a name that he could grow into, and he liked the idea of growing into a big development company despite his current status as a one-man band.

He was a sole trader with a B&Q How to Do It book, which could invariably be found tucked under the driver's seat of his van. This was Andi's bible. This was how Andi did every job back then. Andi was a yes man – any job that came up, he said yes to. The recession of 2007–2008 was underway, and fewer people could afford major home improvement projects.

Andi taught himself to rigidly stick to a budget and look after the pennies. He couldn't charge on par with what bigger companies charged; he had to remain competitive to win jobs. And because he was a yes man, he sometimes took on jobs that he didn't know how to do. But the B&Q book did – the B&Q book which he still has today, which mainly serves as a souvenir, a reminder of where he started, much like my travel diary.

Andi quickly built up a solid local reputation for high-quality workmanship. Acutely aware that he was not a licensed qualified carpenter, Andi fastidiously made sure that every job he did was finished to the best of his ability, even if it meant that he had to be there twice as long or do it all again. Each job had to be perfect, something he still does today. But it meant that he worked until very late every night and all through the weekends and hardly ever saw his family, and when he did, his mind was almost always on the stresses of his job.

In 2009, Andi started to think bigger and got his first extension job. This was a big jump up at the time from the small internal-type works he had been doing. Andi now needed a team around him. He needed to worry about scaffolding, brickwork, roofing, and steelwork, and was taking on much bigger quotes. It seemed the only way to grow his business in the right direction. This growth was full of new challenges, as he was determined to stick to the same standards as he had when on his own. That proved to be far more difficult, the more people he had working around him. He had imagined that, with a team working for him, his life would get much easier, choosing the perfect jobs, with no problems and great, happy customers. He thought that one day he'd retire and go lie on a beach somewhere.

As he took on more and more extensions, growing in size and complexity each time, his team of employed labour and subcontractors was growing too. Meanwhile, my wife's parents were trying to get planning for a house in a sectioned-off piece of their garden. However, there was a restrictive covenant on their title deeds stating that their plot should just be one dwelling. It took some time, but they managed to get the covenant removed and gain planning permission for a good-sized detached house set back and to the side of their property.

It was 2012 and self-build mortgages were relatively rare, as the UK was still recovering from the recession, but Andi decided it was the right time to build his own home. He found a lender that would just about give him enough money, but he needed to invest a percentage up front, £50,000, before the lender would finance the build.

In October 2012, Andi broke ground, using the team that he'd built up around him. It was definitely exciting times for him. He remembers walking around the scaffold every night after work, with the bonfire still raging, watching the lights of the rush-hour traffic on the distant bypass with a warm feeling that he was doing this for his family. He was building for himself now, not someone else.

As I was working for the LED lighting company at the time, I saw an opportunity to gain another customer. I asked him if he needed any lighting for his house and he requested a quote for kitchen lighting. The house was just a slab at this point, so I was working off the plans. Back during my George Wimpey days, I had read house plans all the time. Whilst I couldn't look at a plan and know how to build the house, I was very good at visualising what it would look like in the end. It was as if I were standing in the middle of the finished room. I could picture where best to put the sofa, TV, art, flower pots, beds, lighting, etc.

After quoting Andi for his under-pelmet kitchen lighting, I suggested ways to add lighting throughout his home, more for effect and the look rather than practical. Andi had light tunnels upstairs to bring natural light into his hallway and I thought it would be good to add that idea into his kitchen. Kitchens, mainly on the ground floor, are restricted to light tunnels due to the rooms above, so I had to be creative. Rather than normal down-lighters, I suggested LED panels in the ceiling, which were just becoming popular. These panels were mainly used to replace office lighting in suspended ceilings. I wasn't sure whether they had ever been installed into a kitchen before but I thought they would look like light tunnels. After showing him a sample, he agreed. Andi also installed two strips of LED in the ceiling around his kitchen, one white and one colour-changing strip. It was great for me to get involved in this as I enjoyed the design side of my job. I love to create.

Andi managed to complete the house in seven months and move in by May 2013. The house was about two thousand square feet, with large rooms, a big garden for his three boys, Sonos wireless speakers in each room, and a Control 4 system to switch all of the lighting and sound systems on and off by phone. I had done my part with the lighting design and had enjoyed being involved with a project from the beginning, through to completion. The whole project felt like he had really achieved something, although he had to put £60,000 on several 0% credit cards to finish the house in the end, until the final tranche could be released from the bank on completion.

After that, Andi went back to building extensions for other people. He enjoyed working on people's houses, using their hard-earned savings to build them their dream home, but when they can't afford to move out while the work is being done, and find living in a building site becomes frustrating, it's bloody hard work. It doesn't take long for the novelty of the impending new home to wear off and for clients to lose patience with the ever-present dust. It just added to Andi's stress.

It was during one of these stressful conversions that Andi saw an advert on Facebook on how to get into property investment. Although my dream of starting my own business still lingered, by now I was comfortable in my existing job. I had a company car, I was saving up for my wedding, and life was okay. But working with Andi to design the lighting for his house had stirred something in me.

After the passing of my dad, a lighting design business was an obvious choice to start my own business. I enjoyed lighting and that is what I knew at the time. I started to construct a business plan and gather ideas of what I wanted to do. Andi recommended setting aside enough money to live on during the start-up phase, but I didn't have any money. My income wasn't substantial enough and I had never saved anything.

I thought about the promise I had made to myself, to make my dad proud, and reached out to a few local companies I knew to see if they had any lighting needs. I decided I would call my company Quintessential Lighting Design (QLD).

Then, on 27th December, I got a call from Andi. He told me about the Facebook advert he'd seen, and that he was now listening to an audio book about ways to invest in real estate. Knowing I was keen to start my own business, he wanted to know whether I would be interested in exploring this with him.

I was intrigued. Property was something I was very into, as I had loved what I did for George Wimpey and had a buy-to-let that I owned jointly with my brother, which my nan and grandad had helped us purchase.

I immediately ordered a copy of the book online and read it within days (which is a record for me, as all I'd ever read were autobiographies of business people and sports stars).

Accompanying these books were two free tickets to a three-day property investing seminar in January 2014. Sceptical initially, I listened to everyone onstage. We heard from experts in their preferred property strategy. We discovered that you can get into property investing by using other people's money if you didn't have any of your own. Obviously, this was interesting as it was exactly the position that I was in. Andi and I discussed our options and agreed this was what we wanted to do together, as a business and as a partnership.

I was buzzing. I was ready to go, and I knew things were looking up. I had always wanted my own business and now I had not one but two on the horizon. How had it all happened so fast? Because I decided to do something about it and start.

Remember the Zig Ziglar quote I mentioned in the previous chapter? I hadn't waited until I felt I was great at something to devote myself to it. I just chose to start. Unfortunately, the passing of my dad and grandad is what spurred me to do it, but that moment has shaped my life thus far.

More than ever, I was determined to change my life. Now I had a reason, a motivation.

It is better to fail trying than fail to start.

Secret Tip #2: Don't wait for unfortunate moments in your life to awaken your dream. Start dreaming now and act on them so you can make your family proud while they are around to witness it, and not just in spirit.

Chapter 3 Our First Deal

22-garage site, St James, Northampton

From the first chapter, you may be thinking that the site we had purchased at auction was a risk. Without a doubt it probably was. We had no training in property developments, so we had to learn on the job.

Purchasing a site when you have no experience, no money, and no free time to devote to it might sound crazy to you. Or it might not. The point is that I'm not any different to anyone else. I have the same fears and concerns, many of the same thoughts and emotions. Andi does too.

We both wanted to get into property investing, however, and focusing on property development straight away seemed the right route to go, because of Andi's building background. We debated keeping the properties once we'd finished developing them rather than selling the properties for profit as the majority of investors do. A part of me thought it would be easier to sell them, as my new-build real estate background was in sales, but the thought of holding on to them was appealing.

I did some research and asked a few commercial finance brokers if we could – if it had been done before – and they were very confident in their answers. Yes, it could be done, and, yes, there were lenders available. So we decided to keep the properties as a build-to-rent project, a strategy we adopted and focused on from day one. We didn't know there was such thing as build-to-rent back then. We called it 'build a load of properties and keep them at the end'. I guess build-to-rent has a better ring to it.

Beyond the three-day property seminar that we attended in January 2014, there was no one we knew of who was teaching or promoting property developments, so we had to teach ourselves, to learn by getting on with it and doing a development. This was going to be a huge learning curve. This was going to be a life-changing challenge.

How we did it

How did we structure a deal where we purchased a site at auction, put no money of our own into it, and afford to keep all the units once we'd made all the improvements?

At auction, Andi had £16,000 left in his business account, which was enough to cover the required 10% deposit on the purchase price of £157,000. The remaining £141,000 we thought we could raise from asking people. Quite a bold statement, considering we had no experience borrowing money off people. At auction, you have 28 days to complete a purchase, so we had 28 days to find that £141,000.

We were submitting the site for planning approval for eight 2-bedroom town houses. I created a spreadsheet that predicted a roughly 30% profit:

Purchase Price	£157,000
Development Costs	£600,000
Total Spend	£810,000
Gross Development Value (GDV)	£1,160,000
Profit	£350,000

The first step was to borrow the £141,000 to purchase the plot within 28 days. We put an information packet together and emailed and spoke to anyone we knew who might be interested.

A family friend, and successful businessman, invested £50,000. That left us £91,000 to find. I won't deny it was a struggle. If you have never purchased a property or plot of land from auction before, you are legally required to complete on the purchase within 28 days from the auction date. That is one hell of a challenge when you haven't got any money. It is even harder when you haven't got anyone you can get money from. I didn't have a black book of wealthy contacts that I could call up and ask for money, and neither did Andi.

We had, however, joined a mentorship programme that featured some great people who had been doing property for a while. One of them suggested we consider getting a bridging loan to give us time to find the rest of the finance. Andi and I looked at each other.

A bridging loan?

We had never heard of such a thing. We were buying land, not a bridge! As it turns out, a bridging loan bridges the gap between a purchase and getting longer-term financing.

In the end, we got the finance. To cover the remaining £91,000 required to purchase the plot within the 28 remaining days, we got a bridging loan for £110,000. This also paid back Andi's initial £16,000 borrow from his company account. The completion of the bridging loan took less than two weeks, which put us a day over the 28-day deadline to complete but the auction house were okay with this, as they knew the finance was imminent. We were now the proud owners of a plot of land, with six months to replace the bridging loan with the private finance needed for us to own the land outright. It took us just half that time and consisted of various smaller investments from family and friends. We borrowed four- and five-figure amounts (£3,000, £12,000, £22,000 and so on), until the bridging loan was repaid.

Owning the land outright and unencumbered opened up opportunities from lenders, as they could lend 100% of the build costs and take a first charge over the land as security. The lender that our broker at the time had introduced us to wasn't your everyday development finance lender. It was a peer-to-peer crowdfunding platform, Funding Circle. Funding Circle were known for crowdfunding loans to businesses.

They had a successful, well-established business-lending arm with hundreds of staff. They had only started the property development lending arm of their business in 2014, with different lending criteria. With the business side, you needed to have been trading for a minimum of two years and have a turnover of £50,000 a year. The property side, however, didn't require any trading history or turnover. They were interested only in the deal itself and how it would pay them back.

It seemed like a great way to finance the development costs of £600,000. Funding Circle did their due diligence to make sure it would pay them back before placing the first tranche, or drawdown, on their platform for investors, of which they had thousands.

Funding Circle paid its investors a return of around 6% per annum, charging us 8% per annum, plus a 2% arrangement fee. There were no exit fees or early redemption penalties like there are with most development finance lenders, which made it simpler for us.

By this point, we had raised roughly £165,000 from private investors (friends and family) to cover the land purchase and related fees, plus 100% of the development costs from roughly 9,000 Funding Circle investors, an average investment of £66 per investor.

All we had to do was complete the deal, refinance onto a commercial mortgage, and pay our investors back. (I'll go into the details of this in chapter 9.)

The site had lapsed planning which had expired in 2008 for four flats and four maisonettes, with integral communal corridors, but Andi didn't feel the design made the most of the site. The original planning was also for a gable-ended pitched roof over three storeys. We decided to get rid of the pitched roof and internal communal corridors and designed a scheme, with the help of our architect, for eight two-bedroom town houses, each with their own entrance.

The adjacent blocks of flats at the front of the site were flat-roofed, three-storey, white rendered buildings, so it made sense to mimic that design. To differentiate them from the flats, our architects designed a section of grey cladding between the different houses. The planning was submitted in May 2014 and was granted planning six and a half weeks later, with no amendments. This is fairly quick compared to most planning applications, and it was actually returned before the deadline due date, which is unheard of, these days.

The area we were building in was part of Northampton's Enterprise Zone, which is part of the Alive scheme designed to regenerate the town. The council needed houses, and the fact that we were replacing the former council garages which were an eye-sore was probably one reason that they granted planning so swiftly.

We were to be onsite in September 2014.

White Box Property Solutions Ltd

As I mentioned earlier, the property investment book Andi and I had bought each came with a free ticket to a three-day property seminar, which we attended the following January.

On the final day of the seminar, Andi and I decided to join the mentorship programme to help us get started, as it would provide guidance to make sure we were doing the right things. What we didn't realise back then was that we were the only people in that programme at the time looking at getting into new-build developments, notably the build-to-rent model.

The programme we signed up to was a huge step for me. The only thing I had ever spent thousands of pounds on up until that point was my wife's engagement ring, and even that, a lifetime purchase, was scary, to hand over that amount of money. But when I thought about it, so was the mentorship programme. Spending money on your own education is a lifetime investment. Education is with you for life. It's not doing anything with the education that makes its purchase costly. Putting it to good use, on the other hand, can generate infinite returns on that investment.

I was adamant that I was going to make this education pay for itself so I went for it. (In truth, Andi had to front me the mentorship cost initially, until I could get a credit card to pay for it myself. Remember, I had no money back then. I didn't own a credit card and I had no savings.)

Andi and I put our education into action straight away, looking at the plot in Northampton almost immediately, because that's when that auction was scheduled. If we could have chosen a preferred date, we would probably have asked for it to be six months into our property investment business. Then again, maybe the fact that the auction was being held so soon after we'd begun our mentorship programme was the reason we reacted as we did and took action. Where would we be if we didn't go to that auction? What if the lady who had first purchased the site at auction had actually kept it?

After a few months, we decided to set up a company officially. We had many ideas for naming it, including Red Box Property

Investments, Red Box Property, Andi Lloyd Property, White Box Property Developments, and White Box Investments.

We eventually decided on White Box Property Solutions Ltd., the idea behind it being that the first development we were doing was in essence a white box comprising eight houses. Andi had used Red Box Developments previously and it made sense to tie the companies together, taking a longer-term view.

On the 18th July 2014, White Box Property Solutions Limited was incorporated and my long-awaited business undertaking began with my business partner, Andi. Weekdays were spent at my regular job while weekends and evenings were focused on property. I set up an office at home and started screening property deals, but with my new focus on property, I knew I had to be fair to my employer and hand in my notice fairly soon.

Andi and I analysed each deal together. We were both new to investing so it made sense to work it out as a partnership. I would regularly sit with him at his dining room table, working on figures, assessing a best, worst, and likely case in each deal, and underestimated the end value for comfort. Build costs were left to Andi, as he had experience in this.

We looked at everything from a 'What happens if...' point of view to ensure our end values were underestimated, our build costs were overestimated, and our timescales were extended.

I handed in my notice when we purchased our first property deal, a single mid-terraced house in Kettering that we were looking to turn into a four-bed house of multiple occupancy, an HMO. We managed to purchase this property by borrowing the deposit and Refurb costs from my Nan. It was about £30,000 in total.

White Box Property Solutions Limited was set up but had not done anything yet, as we had purchased the site in St James under our own names. This was something that was advised to us as being our best option back in 2014, as our aim was to keep the properties using the build-to-rent scheme. That was prior to the enactment of Section 24, a tax change introduced on 5th April 2017, that denies landlords permission to deduct the full cost of their mortgage interest payments on rental properties before paying tax. One downside of Section 24 is that it is likely to push quite a few lower-rate taxpayers into higher tax brackets despite their income not having increased. Property developments are able to get around this with the introduction of the SPV (see chapter 4).

Once our first HMO was up and running, our accountant advised us to set up a rental collections company. Green Box Lettings now serves as our in-house letting agency that looks after only our properties and no others. Our portfolio manager looks after our current properties and keeps a look out for new properties that come onto the market.

Following this, we set up Blue Box Property Maintenance, which doesn't do a lot apart from own a freehold of a building. And at the start of 2017, we set up Yellow Box Developments, our first property trading company. It buys land and property for sale, adopting the build-to-sell model. We haven't thought about selling to date, but we have the capacity to start developing to sell, should we elect to go down that route.

That's it for the coloured boxes, for now, although I have visions of grey, purple, pink, black, orange, brown, turquoise, crimson, emerald, teal, and so on.

We have various special purpose vehicles (SPVs) too, for various properties that we now own and are currently developing. (See chapter 4 for more on SPVs).

White Box Property Solutions Ltd is now our property development education company. In 2015, following the completion of our first site, we started helping people get into property developments by showing them how we handled our first development.

Teaching was something we never set out to do, yet, four years on, we have since taught a lot of budding developers how to get started and have seen people go on to make life-changing amounts of money, including a couple of earlier students who are set to profit by about £600,000 on their first deal. It's a great feeling, as Andi and I well know.

Property development

Property development is the process of buying, improving, and selling buildings and land and arranging for new buildings to be built. Property development was to be our primary strategy, and we wanted to use Andi's building company, Red Box Developments, to handle the local projects in Northampton, Kettering, Milton Keynes, and the surrounding areas, which have been a goldmine for us.

Property development ranges from a single house build to a big block of flats, a few houses, to a whole estate. The levels of work involved differ depending on the size of the project, but the model and the concept are similar.

It is often easier and more cost-effective to build three, four, or more houses than it is to build just one, as the same primary contractors are required onsite for each. Think Henry Ford, who swore by the efficiency of assembly-line manufacturing.

For a single house build, a ground worker, electrician, plumber, carpenter, and roofer are most commonly onsite, but apart from maybe the carpenter, the other trades don't need to be onsite the entire time. The ground worker isn't going to hang around to watch the carpet being fitted and the walls being painted;

likewise, the roofers aren't going to stand around twiddling their thumbs, watching the house being built, waiting to put the roof on.

Typically, once the ground worker has finished, they move on to their next job. The same goes for the electrician and plumbers, for example. They will be onsite to do their initial planning and first fix, and then, on a single house build, they must wait for other trades like plasterers to complete their jobs before they can start the second fix.

During this time, they likely go off to other jobs rather than wait around for the plasterers to finish. That really would be like watching plaster dry. As well, the electricians might not be free to immediately return to your site straight away. This will affect your build, as you must then wait for the electrician to come back before starting the second fix.

This can have a domino effect on the whole project, if each trade or operation takes longer than planned. With developments, as we will examine later, time spent onsite costs money. The quicker you build and exit, whether that's to sell or re-mortgage, the better.

However, when it comes to developing a site with multiple plots, the trades can go from plot 1 to plot 2 to plot 3, giving the other trades an opportunity to then do their tasks, before cycling back round to plot 1 to continue their next phase of work. With a multiple build, the electrician hasn't left your site and you are building several houses within a similar time-frame to building just one. A typical, average-sized house takes around 26 weeks to build, from foundations to completion. The project time can vary according to size, spec, and the team you have around you. It is important to get the right people.

In recent months, the Government have highlighted the

importance of property development in an effort to fix Britain's broken housing market. Since the 1970s, there have been on average 160,000 new homes built each year in England. The consensus is that the Government need from 225,000 to 275,000 or more homes per year to keep up with population growth and tackle years of under-supplied stock. The shortfall of new homes is not due to a lack of space to build, as if the country were full of houses. In fact, only around 11% of land in England has been built on. That figure is even lower for residential properties.

The shortfall stems from three reasons, according to the recent housing white paper released in February 2017:[1]

1.There are not enough local authorities planning for the homes they need

2.House building is too slow

3.The construction industry is too reliant on a small number of big developers

The Government are looking to address the above three points in the following way:

1.Have local authorities better plan for the right homes in the right places

2.Increase the speed of house construction

3.Diversify the housing market

It will be interesting to see how the Government intend to implement these approaches in the following years. What we can do is to continue to help the Government build new homes.

---

1   See https://www.gov.uk/government/collections/ housing-white-paper.

If this book inspires just a handful of people to start getting into property development, it will only help our country and its housing supply.

Construction methods

The types of houses being built, and the way they are being built, can be improved, in my opinion. Personally, I think the UK is a bit old school in terms of how houses are built. It is time-consuming, whereas in other parts of the world, different, more efficient construction methods are commonly used.

Different methods of construction include steel frame, although this is admittedly not as common for residential properties, and insulated concrete form (ICF), an efficient method very popular in the US.

One of the fastest building methods is modular construction, also known as pre-fab, or pre-fabricated, where different sections of the building (modules) are constructed at an offsite facility and delivered to the site, at which point assembly is swift. For example, a 2015 article in The Guardian discussed a China-based company claiming to be the fastest construction company in the world after having built a 57-storey building in just 19 days. The building comprised 2,736 modules, which were fabricated four and a half months before construction commenced.[2]

We built our 22-garage site in St James, Northampton, using a modular construction method called SIPs, or self insulated panels. SIPs are a high-performance building system for residential and

---

2   'Chinese construction firm erects 57-storey skyscraper in 19 days', The Guardian, courtesy of the Associated Press, 30 April 2015, https://www.theguardian.com/world/2015/apr/30/chinese-construction-firm-erects-57-storey-skyscraper-in-19-days.

light commercial construction. The panels consist of an insulating foam core sandwiched between two structural facings, typically oriented strand board (OSB).

Although we didn't really know anything about modular construction methods, the reason we chose to use this method was the result of a meeting we had with Barry, a local developer. We initially visited Barry to see if he might be interested in investing in our project – not that he knew that, as we never actually asked him in the end. Instead, he advised us on what to do and how to do it.

We shared with him our plans for the eight townhouses we intended to build in what looked like a block of flats. We had changed the original scheme of flats and maisonettes to these, with four in the front and four in the back, and with no rear door or garden as they were back to back. It was a very simple design, and for our first project, it was a good start. Every house had the same layout.

When Barry saw this, he suggested we looked into SIPs. The benefit of this was not a savings in terms of material costs but in speed and less time required onsite. We knew from doing our calculations that the quicker we could complete the construction, the less we would pay in interest on the loans. This is something the UK should consider in terms of building properties faster but, again, we are still old school here.

It became clear to us that the UK are behind in adopting different methods of construction when it came to refinancing these same eight townhouses using the build-to-rent model, and that is something we now check before we use any different construction method.

About three months before completing the properties, we started the re-mortgage process with a commercial broker who had done some of our HMO refinances a couple of months earlier. Up until that point, I hadn't had to get too involved in the deal. I rarely visited the site, not wanting to get in the way, beyond my role to take the occasional pictures and update our investors.

We were surprised to learn that using SIPs are sometimes problematic for lenders, greatly limiting the number of lenders we could arrange a commercial mortgage with. Eventually, we decided to use Shawbrook Bank, a challenger bank, and not your typical high-street bank. They were competitive and the rates, although higher than some high-streets, were good. They accepted the SIPs construction method and were happy to lend.

The whole refinance progress took longer than anticipated, but that was offset by the speed in which we could build the properties. Plus, we had, as always, over-estimated the timescales we thought it would take to build, as a precaution.

Secret Tip #3: Always speak to a commercial mortgage broker before deciding on your construction method to determine what lenders you will have access to at the end of a project if you are adopting the build-to-rent strategy.

Build-to-rent strategy

Our strategy from day one on this property was build-to-rent, because we wanted to build for investment purposes. We could see the silent compounding effect of retaining properties. The longer we can retain the property in our portfolio, history tells us the more likely the value will increase. Even if the value rollercoasters up and down over a period of years, property almost always ultimately rises in value faster than inflation.

The build-to-rent strategy involves building properties and re-mortgaging them onto either a buy-to-let product or a commercial mortgage, depending on the size of the project. Our model of build-to-rent focuses on building ideally two- and three-bed houses, as we find these to be in greater demand as rentals.

Buying land for the build-to-rent strategy is harder than buying land for the build-to-sell method, as you need to buy at the right price if you expect to pull out all of your money. Typically, most lenders will give you up to 75% mortgage of the site's GDV, the gross development value, the total value of all of the units on the development.

So, a site worth £1 million, for example, might be made up of five houses worth £200,000 each, with the mortgage of 75% coming to £750,000. To leave no money in, you need to make sure that all of your costs are on or below £750,000. That includes the land, the build costs, professional fees, legal fees, etc. — everything. If you can do this, you are left with five houses to rent out individually, with one mortgage covering all five properties, and equity of £250,000. Thus, when looking at a build-to-rent model, the mortgage must cover all costs, with the profit margin 25 percent or above, to ensure you do not leave any money in the deal.

Another factor that will decide whether the development plot that you are looking at will suit the build-to-rent strategy is whether the rent stacks up against the mortgage amount. Recently, the Bank of England Financial Policy Committee (FPC) introduced the 'stress test' for lenders. In simple terms, the lenders need to tighten up on lending, meaning that in order for you to qualify for a mortgage, the monthly rent has to more than cover the monthly mortgage payments to ensure you can keep up with payments. This rate differs depending on whether you are a private landlord or a limited company.

The lenders will stress test the affordability at about 6% interest per annum. This will likely increase or decrease as the Bank of England base rate fluctuates. For private landlords, the rent must cover 140% of the mortgage payments, whereas a limited company's rental income must only cover 125%.

There is a simple calculation to work out how much your mortgage payments would be each month on an interest-only mortgage:

(Mortgage value x interest rate) ÷ 12= monthly mortgage payment

So, for example, if you take out an interest-only mortgage of £150,000 at 6% interest, £150,000 × 0.06 = £9,000 in interest per year. Divide £9,000 by 12 month and you have a monthly interest payment of £750 a month.

Using this example, a limited company must command a rental income of 125%, or at least £940 per month, to qualify for that £150,000 mortgage, while a private landlord must be able to achieve rental income of 140%, at least £1,050.

The build-to-sell model is the more traditional exit strategy with property developments, and where the big developers operate, the likes of Barratt Homes, Taylor Wimpey, David Wilson, Bellway, Bloor Homes, Persimmon, and Bovis Homes, to name a few. It is not as essential to buy land at the right price as it is for the build-to-rent scheme, but it always helps.

With build-to-rent, as I just mentioned, we work on having to secure a profit of 25% in order to leave no money in, whereas with the build-to-sell strategy, paying a higher price for the land simply means you make less profit.

Both strategies have their pros and cons. It is up to you which one you choose, although more and more people are looking to build a portfolio, and so the build-to-rent strategy is becoming increasingly popular.

How to value land

A perception exists that land is – or should be – worth a lot of money. In truth, land's only value is its potential for development. Despite this, when a seller wants to offload land, they tend to overprice it. In a recent survey on our Facebook group, Property Developers Secrets, 66% of participants voted that 'overpriced land' is the biggest bug bear when it comes to property development.

I agree. You could know everything there is about property development, have all the money in the world, and have a super-efficient power team in place but if you can't buy the plot of land at a price that makes sense, then it's a non-starter.

Andi and I have a very effective way to help educate the vendor – and the agents, when necessary – about the price of the land they are selling. But first, it is important to understand that whenever we look to sell something, as humans, we generally price it higher than we hope to get for it, and when buying, we typically pitch our offer lower than what we can afford to pay. That's negotiation.

Some vendors may put a plot of land on the market and hope to get their asking price; others are guided by agents. Some agents don't have a clue as to the real value, so they can inadvertently counsel the vendor to demand a price based on false perception. The vendor will then have this in their heads as the value of their land and it could be way beyond what you can pay.

Having said all this, we don't mind paying what land is worth. It is about making sure you are buying at the right price for your intended use. Don't buy with your heart; buy with your head.

How much you should pay for a plot of land depends on your exit strategy, but a desktop appraisal should be the first step in your calculations.

Desktop appraisals are never the final part of due diligence when doing a development. It is – as it says – a desktop appraisal. What a desktop appraisal does accomplish is it filters out those plots that just don't stack up and are not worth investing further time into.

There are two types of land to value, and each requires a different calculation. The first is land with full planning permission. The second is land that has the potential for planning. This includes land with outline planning or no planning at all.

Valuation of land with planning permission

This is a fairly simple and straightforward calculation, assuming that you are using your own money for the deal: that land value equals the gross development value (GDV) after profit, build costs, and other related costs have been subtracted:

GDV – (Profit + Build Costs + Other Costs) = Land Value

Doing a development with none of your own money does require another component in the calculation, which we'll talk about in a moment. But for now, the first step is to determine the GDV, the gross development value, from which you will work backwards, as the calculation shows above.

Let's use the plot at St James, Northampton, as a working example to show you, using real figures.

To find the GDV of a site that has already been granted planning permission is relatively straightforward, because you already know the number of properties planned for the site and often have drawings available showing the size of the properties. This is important to help you work out your build costs.

The St James site contained permission for eight two-bedroom townhouses at roughly 750 square feet per property, or just under 70 square metres each. (To convert square feet to square metres, divide the number of feet (750, in this case) by 10.764, which gives you 69.7 square metres. To convert square metres to square feet, simply multiply the number of square metres by 10.764).

Next, you need to find out how much comparable properties in the street have sold for. The closer you can find similar properties, the easier it is to accurately calculate. Sites like zoopla.co.uk and rightmove.co.uk provide sale prices and sizes. I prefer to use Rightmove because they show you the actual property listing when it was advertised for sale, including the pictures, which makes it easier to gauge a better comparison. You want to identify properties as close to what you are proposing to build as possible.

In St James, there were no two-bed, three-storey townhouses within a quarter mile radius from our chosen site, so the closest I could find at the time were two-bed terraced houses. But that was sufficient for the desktop appraisal.

The rightmove.co.uk site features a tab that says 'House Prices' at the top, and then, in the dropdown menu, a tab that says 'Sold House Prices'. Click on that.

Enter the street name and town in the search bar and a list of all the properties sold on that street should appear. If none do, then there haven't been any sales on that street for a while. If this is the case, expand the radius of your search to range between a quarter and half a mile – no more, because beyond that is too far away from the site, and could include higher-valued areas or lower-valued areas, where the values will be completely different to the area where you are building. You don't want to get a false reading. This is critical in your appraisals.

If you know the area well, then you may know of an area outside the radius you can look at that contains similar house values, but I would only suggest this if you really know the area.

Once you have a list of recent closing prices, look for the two-bed comparable properties. To see how big the properties are, click on a property from the list to take you into the historical listing. It may tell you the size if there are floor plans, but if it doesn't, don't worry.

Secret Tip #4: If the size of the property is not shown, copy the postcode and note the house name or number. Go to epcregister. co.uk and click 'retrieve report using property address', follow the instructions, and find the property's Electric Performance Certificate (EPC). The certificate will show the property's total floor area in square metres. It's not always 100% accurate, but it's close enough.

Okay, now note all the data on a minimum of three comparable properties and calculate the average property price in the area.

If you can't find any sold properties in your area on Rightmove's website, then you may have to speak to three estate agents in the area to see if they have sold any nearby and ask them to tell you the values. Just be careful that the agents haven't furnished you a for-sale (listing) price as these can sometimes be over-inflated.

I work on sold (closing) prices, as that is the true figure of what it is worth – what the market will bear – rather than what someone wishes to sell for. There is a difference.

If there are different properties in the planning permission, as in flats, two-beds, three-beds, four-beds, etc., then you need to calculate this value for each property type on the site.

Once you have all of the comparable figures, it's time to work out your GDV, what I would call your likely case figure. Your likely case figure is still underestimated to what we think will be the case. With the uncertainty in the market, I would prefer to veer on the side of caution versus hope. (To establish a worst case, deduct 5% from the total GDV, and add 5% to get a best case.)

Work on the likely case and keep this GDV figure to one side.

St James:

Eight 2-bed houses at £145,000 per property
8 x £145,000 = £1,160,000 likely GDV

Next, you need to work out your profit. This is a simple calculation. If you want to make 25% profit, multiply the GDV by 0.25. If you want to clear 30% profit, multiply the GDV by 0.30, and so on. Use the 25% profit calculation for the desktop appraisal.

St James:

GDV of £1,160,000 × 0.25 = £290,000

Now, let's take a quick look at build costs. (I will go into the build costs in a bit more detail, later on.)

Build cost snapshot

Defining precisely how much it will cost to build a house is almost as impossible as declaring how long a piece of string is – there are countless possible answers. With a new build, there is an element of accuracy, but accept that your calculations will never be 100% accurate.

Once you are out of the ground, build costs can be closely calculated. To put it into a simpler context, it's like having a recipe for a cake. You know what you intend to make, what ingredients and the tools are required, and how long and at what temperature it takes to bake. New build is similar. You know what you are making, you know what materials you need, and you know how long it should take to build. However, what happens if someone steals your flour? What contingencies have you in place to offset that loss?

When we started in 2014 we only had Andi's previous experience of extensions and his own house to go by. We worked on an estimate of £100 per square foot, but this figure understandably varies based on different factors.

It varies on location and where you are based in the UK. Houses in London cost way more than properties in Northern England, for example.

It varies based on the specifications of what you intend to put into the property. If you are going for a high-end finish, for example, then it will cost you more per square foot.

It also varies based on where you buy your materials and what buying power you have. Maybe a bigger site can reduce the build costs by buying in bulk. (There are different buying groups available to help you buy at bulk prices for smaller sites.)

One thing is for sure: you need to do your homework first and find out how much, as closely as you can, it costs per square foot in your area. There are ways to find this information, such as approaching your local builders merchants for a list of the builders who regularly build larger developments. It is worth speaking to the builders in your area to see at what costs they are building.

The specification of what you are building ultimately determines the build cost price per square foot. Getting this wrong could seriously alter the deals you look at. Your due diligence will be wasted by inaccurate figures, so it's critical to first research how much it costs to build homes in your area, and at what specification.

There are online estimating platforms which are pretty accurate, as they work on localised costs for your area. When items are purchased through some of the builders merchants, it feeds back to the estimators whose prices change regularly to give you a reasonably accurate figure – as accurate as is possible, that is. If you provide the estimators with a plan of the property you intend to build, as detailed as possible, and an elevation, they can give you a very detailed breakdown of the material costs and quantity necessary to build the property, and the associated labour costs.

For this example, we will use a cost estimate of £100 per square foot to illustrate how we worked out the cost of the land at St James.

We start by taking the total size of all of the properties in the development and add them together. Next, we multiply this number by the price per square foot in the site's area. This gives you a guide to how much you should expect to budget for the build of all the properties on your site. This doesn't include certain factors but I will explain what to expect and not expect to be included in the build costs.

St James:

8 two-bed houses at 750 square feet each

Total size: 8 units × 750 = 6,000 square feet

6,000 sq. ft. × £100/sq. ft. = £600,000 estimated build cost

So, now we have the GDV (£1,160,000), the desired 25% profit (£290,000) and the rough build costs (£600,000).

While this desktop appraisal doesn't factor in all of the costs, it's about getting a ball-park figure to quickly assess a given deal on a plot of land, eliminating deals that are not viable, based on the asking price.

The other costs that we could factor in at this point, if you know them, for sites being sold with planning include:

Stamp duty costs (which can only be worked out once you have negotiated a land purchase price)

Community Infrastructure Levy (CIL) costs

Section 106 costs

Roads

Services

Professional fees

Legal fees

Cost of development finance

Demolition costs (if any)

Surveys

and so on…

If you know the costs of any of the above, factor them into your 'other costs' section and total them up.

Unless you have a load of money in the bank, you will more than likely use development finance for the construction. This comes at a cost, as lenders lend money to make money. When borrowing development finance, there are various fees and rates available. As an average, we work on a 10% interest per year figure. Some lenders offer lending at 7% interest a year but tack on a 2% arrangement fee. An arrangement fee generally ranges between one and three per cent, and while some lenders charge it, others don't.

Some lenders have an exit fee. This is also a percentage of the loan amount, but it can sometimes be a percentage of the final GDV amount, so check with your commercial broker as to what, if any, additional fees lenders may charge. Not all lenders charge an exit fee. If they do, it is also worth noting whether the exit fee is calculated based on the loan amount or the GDV amount.

We work on an average of 10% per annum for the desktop appraisal. If a project will take 12 months to build, then we would expect to pay 10% interest. If the project is an 18-month project, then we would expect to pay 15% interest over that 18-month period. If the development is 24 months, then the total interest we'd expect to pay would be two times that annual figure, or 20% interest.

When we worked out the cost of development finance for our St James development, we predicted that the development would take 12 months to build and six months to refinance, so 18 months in total. Therefore, we worked on a total interest payment of 15% for the duration of the development.

To work out the borrowing costs of this, we take the entire build cost and multiply it by 0.15 to calculate what 15% of the costs work out to be. This then gets added to the 'other costs' section

St James[3]

Build costs = £600,000

£600,000 x 0.15 (15%) = £90,000 of interest

The interest figure is overestimated using this quick calculation, which is a good thing. With developments, things can go wrong and budgets sometimes need to be stretched, so you need to have contingencies built into your calculations. This way of calculating the interest adds in a margin to cover some natural contingencies, because we have assumed that we will borrow 100% of the build costs from day one.

This will not be the case when you draw down development finance, as it is drawn down in tranches, so the total build costs will be split into various payments, at different times during the development stage. You only pay interest when you draw down the development finance.

For example, the £600,000 build costs for St James could be split over four tranches, say, £150,000 each. The first £150,000 is drawn down to begin the development and has 18 months to go, i.e., 15% worth of total interest payable on £150,000, which equates to around £22,500.

Five months later, the next tranche of £150,000 is drawn down, which has 13 months to go and 11.2% worth of interest (roughly £16,500). Five months later, the third lot of £150,000 is drawn down, with eight months to go, around 7% worth of interest, or £10,500 payable. The final drawdown of £150,000 is taken with just three months to go and only 2.5% of interest payable

---

3   We didn't include stamp duty and there were no Section 106 or CIL payments to make.

(£3,750).

In the tranche scenario, rather than calculating a straight 18 months of interest (£90,000) that we calculated in the desktop appraisal, the interest we would expect to pay would be about £53,250, By using the £90,000 figure in our estimate, we've built in a contingency of £36,750, about 6% of the total build costs.

There are other ways we build in natural contingencies, which I will explain further on. The interest that accrues throughout a development is rolled up and payable on completion of the development project.

Returning to our St James desktop appraisal, we can now do the following land value calculation, subtracting profit, build costs, and other costs from the GDV to get what I call the gross land value:

£1,160,000 GDV – (£290,000 profit + £600,000 build costs + £90,000 other costs) = £180,000 gross land value

This, in theory, is what you could pay for the land if you had your own money. But we didn't have our own money in 2014. So, we needed to find out how much we could pay for the land and factor in the cost of borrowing all the money to purchase the land from private investors from day one. If we added the interest of borrowing this from the gross land value figure, then the interest we accrue will come out of our profit, which then reduces our profit margin and could eventually result in our having to leave money in the deal.

To work out the true land value, we need to first understand how long we would need to borrow the money, so we can work out how much to factor in to cover the interest payable to our investors.

Working on a plot with full planning is, as I mentioned before, easier to calculate, as one doesn't have to factor in an additional period of time for the planning process. For St James, we added four months to the project length. That's 12 months for the build stage, six months for refinancing, and an additional four months at the beginning of the development, before starting the build stage, to make sure we negotiate a long enough loan term from our investors to cover the entire duration. In the case of St James, this meant a 22-month loan term from our investors, giving them a 10% return per year on their investment.

While each deal will vary based on the amount we can offer our private investors, for the desktop appraisal we work on 10% per year, again for simplicity. That 22 months' worth of interest at 10% per year, which comes to roughly 18% overall.

To work out how much I need to deduct from the land value to factor in the cost of borrowing money from private investors, I simply calculate 18% of the gross land value of £180,000:

£180,000 × 0.18 = £32,400 and deduct this from the land value:

£180,000 - 32,400 = £147,600

This is the net land value, the amount you can justify paying for the land after having factored in the cost of borrowing all the money for the purchase, the build costs, and the cost of borrowing the development finance.

There is another small contingency figure added to this part of the appraisal, as 18% of a larger figure that is deducted is naturally a higher number than adding 18% of a lesser figure.

Realistically we will pay 18% worth of interest on the £147,600 net land value figure.

£147,600 x 0.18 = £26,568

£147,600 + £26,568 = £174,168

A one-step method for this same calculation is to multiply £147,600 by 1.18 (118%).

That provides an added £5,832 worth of contingency, which would cover things like legal fees and any stamp duty. (No stamp duty is assessed on any commercial purchase under £150,000.)

We managed to complete the entire site at a cost of around £106 per square foot, i.e., £638,000, based on a 6,000-square-foot property. And as the townhouses were, in reality, slightly under 750 square feet apiece, our budget of £600,000 was about right.

Asking price

Following the desktop appraisal, you want to categorise your workings against the asking price of the land.

If the net land value is within 10% of the asking price, or above the asking price (this happens occasionally), categorise it as a green lead.

If the net land value is 11–30% lower than the asking price, classify it as an amber lead.

If the net land value is less than 30% of the asking price, that gets classed as a red lead and should be set aside – but not forgotten. Remember, the figure you have worked out is what you can justify paying for the land (in theory, subject to further due diligence) to make it work. It is not the price you made up to get a cheap deal.

Always buy with your head, and not with your heart. Don't chase a site simply because you like it. Buying at the right price is key to a successful development project.

The idea of noting your calculation against the asking price is to identify what sites you should look into further. It allows you to do further full analysis on the sites that seem to stack up in relation to the asking price.

If the net land value is within 10% of the asking price, then the negotiations shouldn't be too hard. But it is important to understand that there are other points to consider regarding the site, not just what it is worth, such as the full site appraisal, other costs, and the site's deliverability. The site could cost you as little as £1, but if you can't build on it for whatever reason, or you can't get planning, that's £1 wasted. Now, what if you calculated that it was worth £1 million? If it's not buildable or planning eligible, that's a lot of money to waste.

Net value of land without planning permission

To work out the net land value of a site without planning requires a bit more work.

In theory, land without planning is worth the net land value, as calculated above, minus the amount of money it takes to get the plot of land to a stage where planning permission is granted.

This is where members of your power team can help you. Experienced developers may be able to gauge how many units they can fit into a plot of land but it is better to source the expertise of your power team, such as your planning consultant and/or architect, for a more accurate estimate, who will look at the council's local development plan or development proposals map.

The map is called different things by different councils, but each council has a map or guide as to where they need housing and is set out in their development plan. Other factors that will determine what you can get on the site is the character of the surrounding properties, the location, whether there are TPOs (Tree Preservation Orders) on the site, if it is located in a flood zone area and the severity, whether it is in an area of natural beauty, and so on.

Once you have a net land value, you must factor in the cost of going through the planning application – the cost of having plans drawn up to get to the planning stage. When you have those costs, deduct them from the net land value, as you are required to pay for them.

Currently, the cost per dwelling to apply for full planning is £462. This is just the cost to apply for full planning permission, and doesn't include fees charged by planning consultants and architects.

There may be other costs to consider in getting a plot of land through planning, which itself is never a guarantee. This could have an impact on your borrowing costs from private investors, as planning approval would extend the period of time that elapses before you can start developing the site, and so that needs to be considered.

Contingency purchase offer

One way to mitigate your risk of not getting planning after contracting to purchase a site is to make your offer subject to planning approval. We have purchased sites where one of the conditions in the contract was that if we exchanged (paid a deposit) prior to getting planning, which generally is 10% of the purchase price, the deposit would be 100% refundable. This way, the only money invested to pursue the plot of land would be the cost of the planning application, plus the time spent by our power team. This is the at-risk money, and can be reduced with a decent planning consultant.

The desktop appraisal is a great way to calculate a rough cost of the land. Note that you should always have a full site appraisal to confirm the site works before any legal contributions on the site.

The full site appraisal is important, as we'll see in a moment. To do a full site appraisal you need to look into the following:

Cost of Section 106, if any

Cost of CIL, the community infrastructure levy, if any

Effect on affordable houses, if any

Cost of roads and access

Title plan, right of ways, ownerships Sloping sites (every metre difference in height generally adds 1% to the build costs)

Tree Protection Orders (if they would affect the design of the site) Any existing covenants on the site

Searches

Flood risk assessments

Sales assessment and viability

Contaminated land – cost of remedial work

Marketing costs

Agency fees

What, if any, demand exists for the area

If employing a build-to-rent strategy, whether the rental income can adequately cover the mortgage payments (by a minimum of 125%)

What, if any, planning conditions need to be addressed (even if a site with planning approval appears straightforward, there may be some costly and time-consuming conditions to address before you can commence a build)

A well-established property investor brought us an opportunity in Cumbria, as they knew that we were currently developing there, along with Northamptonshire, Buckinghamshire, and Devon.

The site was a fantastic plot in a town with great industry and businesses, and had the potential to house up to 80 units. As you may imagine, the figures looked amazing. The GDV was around £18 million, with a profit of around £5 million. On paper, it was a great site.

It was way beyond where we were at the time, both in cost and size, but we had just increased our team, and our Project Manager, who possessed 12 years of experience with one of the UK's biggest house builders, was used to building 80–100 homes a year, so we thought long and hard about taking on the development. We had quite a bit of financial backing at this time, which helped.

Obviously, this is not the kind of project we would have considered at the beginning of our property development business, and it was certainly a huge step up – maybe a step up too many? But why couldn't we do it, we asked ourselves.

We went further into the due diligence of the site and looked into the town and whether it could cope with a further 80 houses. After all, it is all well and good to build 80 houses, but if you can't do anything with them, they become nothing more than a huge burden.

Imagine if you had built 80 homes but couldn't sell them! Think about all of the finance you would still need to pay back. How would you do it? It would be a very costly mistake.

With the site seeming to stack up and the money becoming available to do the project, we did some more due diligence. During our analysis, we discovered that the town had only sold 14 houses in the previous 12 months. (A great way to check this is online, via Zoopla. (If you go onto Zoopla, there is a tab called 'House Prices' and the dropdown menu offers 'UK area stats'. This will give you all of the sales from the area, going back 20 years).

As you can imagine, only 14 houses having sold in 12 months was a deal breaker for us. The town would definitely not cope with a further 80 homes. So, we dismissed it.

This was a great decision for us, as not only did it make us think bigger and give us the confidence to look at larger sites but it built a significantly higher level of trust and confidence between us and the well-established property investor, which we since went on to do other deals with. My point is that you shouldn't try to make a deal work because the numbers look good. Make sure you do your full due diligence.

Secret Tip #5: Once you have done your desktop appraisal, make your offer subject to planning (if applicable) and subject to full site appraisal. This way, your offer is in and the agent/vendor is aware that you are interested. Sometimes, the full appraisal can take a few days, so it is important to have your foot in the door. Following your full appraisal, you can amend your offer with reason.

Chapter 4 Special Purpose Vehicles (SPVs)

It is common practice nowadays to form a special purpose vehicle (SPV) when starting a property development. This is normally in the form of a limited company or limited partnership. I am neither an accountant nor a tax specialist, so please understand that I am not advising you on what you should do, or how. Be sure to seek appropriate professional advice before venturing into any property development.

I want to share with you an extract from The Schmidt Tax Report[4] that highlights the benefits of an SPV for property developments. The Schmidt Tax Report is a fantastic resource for explaining tax in plain English. You can visit the website here: https://www. schmidtreport.co.uk.

It says:

Reducing property tax with a special purpose vehicle

Property development is absolutely in fashion at the moment, with the economic recovery in full swing and a general shortage of places for people to live. There's no doubt that, for those with the enterprise, skills, and money to undertake developments, this can be a good way to get rich.

Thanks for the lecture, you might say, but what's all this got to do with tax? Surely we just have to pay our tax on the property development profits, if we make them, and try to look cheerful?

The following case study illustrates, using wholly plausible facts that I personally have seen time and time again in practice, how important it is to plan sensibly for tax when undertaking a

---

4   Reprinted with permission.

development.

The difference between the result for Rock and Sandy, in the examples below, is truly eye-watering, as you will see.

Sandy

Over the years, Sandy has painfully built up a cash balance in his trading company. He's not a property developer by background but a widget manufacturer. By saving money up within his limited company, he's managed to get to the point where the company is sitting on surplus cash deposits, which he doesn't need for the business, of £500,000.

I don't know how many of you, my readers, actually do make widgets for a living, but for those of you who don't I can tell you it's very hard work. What with all the cheaply manufactured widgets flooding the market from China, and ever more oppressive labour laws and 'rights' for workers, the margins are very tight for making these little items, and it takes a long time to build up reserves of half a million pounds.

Sandy's next-door neighbour, Lucky, seems to have a much easier life. Every now and again he finds a plot on which planning is available, or may be granted, to build a small estate of houses, and Lucky seems to devote quite a small proportion of his time to this activity, and always has a new car to drive to the airport for his long Caribbean holidays.

Sandy's not a quick thinker (as you will see from what follows), but it eventually dawns on him that doing a development may be a way of shortcutting this slow and laborious process of building up a retirement fund by manufacturing widgets.

One morning the doorbell rings. It's his next-door neighbour Lucky come to borrow the lawnmower because one of his gardeners has broken theirs.

The two men get talking. After about half an hour of chitchat about the weather and business, Lucky falls silent for a moment, gazing out of Sandy's back window at the vast (and rather wild) expanse of his back garden.

"You know what I'd do, don't you?" says Lucky. "I'd talk to the council about planning permission for building two or three houses at the bottom of your garden. You obviously don't need such a large plot."

This is certainly a tip from the horse's mouth. "This man knows what he's talking about," thinks Sandy. So, after talking it through with his wife, he starts doing the sums. The land costs him nothing, planning and building costs, after a lot of head scratching and consultation with a builder, he assesses at up to about £500,000. He can just about squeeze three houses on the site, each of which will net him £300,000, total £900,000. So he looks to make a clear profit of £400,000.

How beautifully it all fits into place! He's got the £500,000, sitting there in the bank account of his limited company, and so he doesn't even need to borrow from the bank. In 18 months' time, so the builder assures him, he could be richer to the tune of the £400,000 profit, which would take him four or five years to earn from the day job.

Sandy has a spring in his step when he goes into the office on Monday morning. He calls in his bookkeeper and tells him to make up a cheque, payable to Sandy, for £500,000, and to do the necessary dividend paperwork to make this legal.

He's quite acute in some ways is Sandy (although not as far as tax is concerned), and he's worked out that rather than paying a lot of money to a large building company to do the work (for which he duly gets planning permission), he could supervise the tradesmen himself, and buy all the materials himself. That way, he avoids paying the builder a 25% profit margin and keeps the profit for himself: magic. After the usual hassle, he manages to get a credit account registered in his name with the local builders merchants. Building begins.

Everything goes according to plan (well, this is a made up case study) until the time comes to market the houses. For some reason, whether to do with a temporary blip in the world economy or because a planned expansion of the nearby town has been shelved indefinitely, he finds it difficult to sell the three 'executive homes' that now grace the plot at the end of his garden. The estate agent assures him they will fetch the £300,000 each that he had originally planned, but that it's a buyer's market at the moment. (Everyone knows that it's always a buyer's market if you are a seller and always a seller's market if you are a buyer.)

On the other hand, the estate agent is able to provide some rather more practical help, and manages to find tenants to occupy the houses, on six-month tenancies, until such time as they do sell. In the end the houses do all sell, but not until after the tenants have renewed their six-month leases three or four times.

The tax nightmare

All's well that ends well, then. Well, not exactly. The first unexpected problem that rears its head is when, some months after building has begun, Sandy's accountant writes him a letter (he's too frightened to telephone) in which he tells Sandy that his tax bill, payable on 31st January, is £150,000. Sandy is in despair, until he realises there is an unused overdraft facility in the company, which would enable him to take this money out of the firm by way of a further dividend, in order to pay his tax.

In due course, the £150,000 is going to give rise to another higher-rate income tax bill, of course, and at the end of the day the tax spiral operates in good earnest. The accountant works out that the total tax he ends up having to pay is arrived at by grossing up the £500,000 at his effective 30% higher-income tax rate. That is, the total cost of taking the money out of the company ends up being £214,000 or thereabouts.

The whole idea of building houses at the bottom of the garden now seems much less attractive, now Sandy knows the tax downside. But worse is to come.

After all of the costs have been paid to the solicitors and estate agents, Sandy banks the £400,000 profit in his personal bank account and breathes a sigh of relief – premature, because the accountant has another bombshell for him. Because of all of the other income he has taken from the company, both to live on and to fund tax bills, he's in the 45% rate of income tax, together with national insurance at 2%, making an overall rate of 47%.

So Sandy has to wave goodbye to nearly half of his £400,000 profit, that is, £188,000.

Then the VATman arranges a visit.

With all the inevitability of a Greek tragedy, where the hammer blows of fate strike down the hero one after the other, the VATman points out that he has reclaimed tax of nearly £100,000 on the building costs, on the basis that, as everyone knows, someone building new houses can 'zero rate' the proceeds. Zero rating is a very strange concept of tax, where tax is prima facie chargeable, but at a zero percentage rate. The effect of this is that new-home builders can claim back all of the VAT charged to them on building materials, etc., and not have to pay any VAT on their ultimate sale proceeds.

The problem is, if you end up letting out the completed houses, rather than selling them, as Sandy was forced to do by the market conditions, you've suddenly got exempt income rather than zero-rated income, being rents from letting out the houses.

VAT is a bad tax to be exempt from, because the effect is that any VAT you have reclaimed, thinking that your outputs are going to be taxable, gets clawed back by the VATman.

The VATman, according to his lights, treats Sandy fairly. He doesn't ask for the whole of the VAT back, because the houses were, eventually, sold. However, he agrees a proportion with Sandy's accountant which, together with interest and penalties, amounts to about £40,000 – which Sandy has to take out of the company, pay higher-rate tax on, etc., etc.

If anyone thinks this story is contrived, and nobody could possibly be as unlucky as my fictional hero, I can correct them. These are all situations that I have seen happen in real life.

Let's tot up the total tax bill at the end of this unfortunate saga. First of all, there's the higher-rate income tax on taking the money out of the company to fund the development: £214,000 at the end of the day. Then there's the 47% effective 'tax' rate on the profit: £188,000. Then the last-minute sting in the tail being the cheque on account of VAT, together with 'extras': £50,000. In total, the taxman is richer to the tune of £452,000 as a result of Sandy's venture. The only one who has got rich quick is George Osborne.

Rock

OK, you can put away the box of Kleenex now. Rock is an

individual who thinks about what he's doing before he does it and, in particular, thinks about the tax effects of what he's doing. On the face of it, he ought to fare as badly as Sandy, because, by an incredible coincidence, his basic financial situation is exactly the same as Sandy's. He too has a plot to develop at the bottom of his garden, and in his case the three houses will come in at a total overall cost of £500,000 and yield £900,000 net proceeds, giving him a profit of £400,000. Rock also has a limited company with £500,000 'spare' cash in it.

There is only really one big difference between Rock and Sandy: Rock asks his accountant/tax adviser how he should structure his development.

The tax adviser suggests setting up a limited company as a special purpose vehicle (SPV) to carry out the development. This is funded not by way of taking a dividend out of Rock's manufacturing company, which is then put into the SPV, but by way of an interest-free intercompany loan to the SPV. The SPV doesn't take ownership of the land but acts as a kind of captive building contractor for Rock, who continues to hold the land personally.

Rock is as switched on as Sandy in the financial sense, and he has also worked out that by managing the development himself he can avoid paying a profit element to some external building contractor/ developer. So the SPV goes and gets an account at the builders merchant, contracts with all of the tradesmen and charges Rock personally for its services. Effectively, the whole profit from the development goes into the SPV, because it charges its costs with a mark-up.

At the end of the day, when the houses are ultimately sold, the SPV company is left with all or virtually all of the £400,000 'profit' on the development in its own bank account. Rock himself makes little or no profit, certainly not enough to pay any substantial amount of tax on.

Assuming for simplicity's sake that the company realises the full £400,000 profit, it will obviously have to pay corporation tax on that profit, at 20%. So the company has a liability of £80,000: which you will notice is the first tax liability that has had to be paid in this much happier story. Rock then decides to put the SPV into liquidation as its commercial purpose is at an end. He takes out the £320,000 cash remaining in the company's bank account, and pays capital gains tax (CGT), which we will assume is on the full amount because he is using his CGT annual exemption elsewhere. CGT on winding up a trading company, which has been trading for at least a year, is generally eligible for entrepreneurs' relief, so the applicable rate is no more than 10%: giving a further personal tax bill for Rock of £32,000.

So the total tax that has been paid all along the line here is £112,000.

When the VATman visits, which he does just after leaving Sandy a smouldering ruin, he gives the SPV a clean bill of health. It has zero-rated its services to Rock, quite correctly, because these are the services of a building contractor constructing new dwellings. So the VAT on all of the costs is correctly reclaimed and the VATman has nothing to claw back in this case.

The overall result is that the taxman has had £452,000 from Sandy and less than a quarter of this, £112,000, from Rock. The one thing I should point out, to be rigorously fair between these two scenarios, is that Sandy has, of course, had the benefit of moving the £500,000 cash out of corporate ownership and into his personal ownership, at a substantial cost in terms of tax. But the old saying is "A tax deferred is a tax saved" and it may be that Rock never has to pay anything similar on the possibly distant date when he takes the £500,000 out permanently for his personal use: or the tax rate he does eventually pay may be very much less than 30%.

Indeed, it's more likely that Rock, with his pleasant experience of dealing with property developments, will plough the money back again into another development in future. Sandy is much more likely to go back to manufacturing widgets after his experience.

From the above case scenarios, you can see that the pros heavily outweigh the cons. Whilst a fictional scenario, it explains the importance of setting up an SPV for a development. An SPV is also a great way to borrow money from development finance lenders. You can also bring private investors into the SPV more easily.

This next section has been written with the help of Alan, who writes regularly in the Schmidt Tax Report (www.schmidtreport. co.uk), and is the author of The Entrepreneurs' Tax Guide, which contains a very good chapter on property development.

The impact of taxation

The way your property development will be taxed depends on which side of a crucial and very important line your development falls. The easiest way to describe this line is by asking the question, 'Are you developing properties so that you can hold on to them for rent, or are you developing them to sell?'

Of course, there's the possibility that you might answer this question with 'I don't know'. If this is the answer, we will consider your position further on.

Developing to retain

If yours is a long-term game, the choice of a Special Purpose

Vehicle (SPV) will be different than if you are developing to sell in the short term. A lot of people set up a limited company as an SPV without giving the tax implications much thought. It's true that a limited company has the advantage, or apparent advantage, that the rents you receive will be taxable at corporation tax rates which, as we write, are 19%. This could be quite a bit less than the personal income tax rates you would pay if you held the property personally. However, there is a 'sting in the tail' which relates to the capital gains treatment if you were to ever sell any of the properties (as ultimately, of course, they must be sold).

This is the so called 'double charge to tax', under which the company would pay tax on the gain in value of the property between construction and sale, and then the shareholders of the company would pay a second layer of tax on getting the money out, either by way of dividend or by winding up the company. Very often – indeed, more often than not – this can result in a significantly greater amount of tax on the ultimate sale than if you'd simply owned the property personally.

And it isn't necessarily just a simple trade-off between lower taxes on income on the one hand and higher taxes on gains on the other. That's because personal ownership isn't necessarily completely inconsistent with some of the rental profits being charged at company rates. You could, for example, have a limited company which makes a charge for running the portfolio. This would reduce the amount of the rents chargeable to income tax, at the expense of profits ending up in the company, where they pay 19%.

For those who develop to retain, an interesting and more sophisticated ownership structure is the limited liability partnership (LLP). This could have various family members and even friends as members and enable you to spread the income tax load of the rents amongst various people.

Developing to sell

If you are looking to sell the resultant dwellings in the short term after completing them, your choice of SPV is likely to be a limited company. This is because the profit from a property development of this kind is taxable as income rather than as capital gain. Unlike capital gains tax, which has a top rate of 28%, tax on income has an effective top rate of 47% (including class 4 national insurance), and this can be a very painful amount to lose from your development profits. Limited companies pay tax at the same rate, whether you are talking about gains or income, that is, at the 19% rate we've already mentioned. So, there's an immediate, and perhaps very significant, tax advantage in using a limited company if you're developing to sell.

Of course, that's not the whole story, because you have the question, once again, of what happens to the money in the company after it's paid its corporation tax?

If you are a one-off developer, you might well decide to wind up the company after doing the development. The cost of this is another 10% tax, being capital gains tax under the 'entrepreneurs' relief' code. Even paying this second layer of tax, though, only gives you a total overall tax charge of 27% (corporation tax at 19%, plus capital gains tax at 10% on the 81% that's left). You're very unlikely to be able to match this as a direct personal trader, and your tax could nearly be twice as much.

On the other hand, if you're looking to do further property developments, the winding up route isn't probably a very good idea for technical tax reasons. But the money is available within the company to conduct your next development with, and the important point to note is that you've only haemorrhaged 19% of the profits from the first development before using the remainder to fund your second development.

VAT

VAT is an area where you can trip yourself up in doing property development if you plan to sell but then, for perhaps commercial reasons, retain any of the completed dwellings instead – even if only temporarily.

Here is the nightmare scenario: Just as Sandy chose to do in the example earlier in this chapter, you undertake the development work yourself, because you don't feel you need an overarching contractor to do the development for you. As a result, you incur VAT on various expenses, including professional costs and builders materials. You reclaim all of these because, as is well known, a new development of houses and flats is 'zero rated' for VAT. What this means is that you don't have to charge any VAT to the person buying your new house, flat, etc., but you can nevertheless reclaim all the VAT you incurred in doing the building.

This is all very well until there is a change of plan, and you decide to hang on to some or all of the developed dwellings after they're completed. (Remember Sandy, who couldn't find buyers right away and was forced to rent his new-builds in the interim?) For technical reasons, this results in a clawback of all the VAT you've incurred, because rents you receive from tenants are not 'zero rated' but are 'exempt'. (VAT is a peculiar example of a tax, as mentioned earlier, as it is bad to be 'exempt from').

How to avoid this? The answer is that even if you're not using an overall building contractor to do the work, you can set one up for yourself, just like Rock's tax advisor, in the earlier example, suggested he do. That is, you can set up a development company in which you own 100% of the shares, and this would register for VAT, and reclaim all of the tax on materials, etc. The company then invoices on to you as the property owner but invoices without VAT because the work of the company is zero rated. So, even if you then let out the property, you haven't incurred any input VAT yourself, as property owner, for HMRC to claw back.

The don't knows

For those who aren't quite certain at the outset of a development whether to sell or hold on to the developed dwellings, probably the best way to hedge your bets in this situation is to have the same dual SPV structure as the person who has decided to retain the property. The building contracting company, of course, guards against the danger of VAT being clawed back. But it also potentially shelters the profits of the development.

In the vanilla scenario, where we are just using the development company to avoid a clawback of VAT, the development company would be unlikely to make much or any profit, because doing so would generate a tax charge. However, there is nothing stopping it making a profit, by marking up the amount it charges to you as the property owner by a reasonable amount. This would be advantageous, in all probability, if you then go on to sell the property, because the costs (including profit mark-up) charged to you by the contracting company are deductions against the profit on which you then pay income tax.

Alan Pink FCA ATII is a specialist tax consultant who operates a bespoke tax practice, Alan Pink Tax, from offices situated in Tunbridge Wells. Alan advises on a wide range of tax issues and regularly writes for the professional press. Alan has experience in both major international plcs and small local businesses and is recognised for his proactive approach to taxation and solving tax problems. Alan can be contacted on (01892) 539000 or email: alan.pink@alanpinktax.com. His book, The Entrepreneur's Tax Guide, is on sale from Head of Zeus for £20, or from all good book shops.

Ready, Fire, Aim, Do it! Make it Happen! Action Counts. No one ever sat their way to success. –Tom Peters

Chapter 5 Power Team

Steering your way through property developments is like flying a jumbo jet. Just because you know how to drive a car doesn't mean you would just turn up at an airfield one day, never having even seen the inside of a plane, jump into the captain's seat, turn on the engine, and expect to take off successfully. For one, you wouldn't know what to do – you wouldn't know what button to press, or which dial to turn. It would be a disaster, and a very costly one too.

Property development is a bigger business than your standard buy-to-let property investment. It's riskier but can be more rewarding. Returning to the jumbo jet analogy, buy-to-lets are your car. You learn the basics of getting into a car and driving with help from someone who has done it before. Once you have learnt the basics and had a little practice, it becomes second nature. You can quite easily jump in your car, turn the engine on, and go. No checks, no thought, just drive off.

When piloting a jumbo (not that I have ever done it, but it was one of the many professions I aspired to as a kid), you have a set procedure, a standard checklist to follow before take-off. You have a team around you to assist you: the co-pilot, a grounds team, cabin crew, air traffic control, and so on. Let's put this into context with a development.

The jumbo jet is your development, the instrument you intend to operate.

Your destination is your exit strategy, the end goal.

The captain is you – you control each step of the journey, how you reach the destination.

The air traffic controllers are your mentors; they overlook what you're doing.

The passengers are your family, friends, house, income, health, etc. You need to protect them, to make sure they arrive at the destination safely.

Your co-pilot is your business partner (unless you are flying solo), who is there to assist you and help you through the journey.

The ground team and the cabin crew comprise your power team.

Before you take off, you must first learn how to fly. You need to be taught, you need to understand the mechanics of how to get to your destination, and you need to understand the possible consequences of your chosen flight path and any deviations you may find yourself having to take.

You need to know what to look out for, like rough weather patterns, or birds that might get sucked into your engines. You need to know how to take off and how to land, and you need to understand what it takes to get you to the finish (education, mentors). This book serves as your introductory training manual and, if you will, your flight simulator.

Once you have learnt how to fly, it's down to you to take you there. As you take your place in the captain's seat, you do your flight checks first. You check that everything is safe, that conditions are optimal and all mechanics are operational (solicitor, accountant), before taking off.

Once you have decided it is safe to proceed, and that all of your checks will get you safely to your destination, it's time to engage (quantity surveyor).

Your grounds crew ensure the plane is fully fuelled (joint venture partners, commercial finance broker), verify the tires are inflated (insurance broker), and confirm that the externals of the plane are good to go (planning consultant, architect).

You give air traffic control the nod that you are ready, and they respond that you will be clear for take-off once they have checked the clearance (mentors).

Much of the rest will be up to you. You still have to safely guide it to the finish in order to land. Along the way there may be turbulence. You will need to react to it and control it; otherwise you put your passengers in danger. If you fail to touch down, then it is costly.

You consult air traffic control (mentors) as you enter new territory. You consult your co-pilot (business partner) along the way and make sure you agree that you are still on the right path. Meanwhile, you cruise along, getting closer to your destination. Your crew continue to make sure that everything is okay in the cabin along the way (architect, builder). And as you come in to land, you speak to air traffic control (mentors) again, and they give you the clearance to land.

Touch down!

You've done it. You've landed. Your passengers are delighted and so are you. You have just completed a development – but not on your own. Your team have helped you the entire time. Your responsibility is to make sure the team do what they need to do to help you to reach your desired destination.

Much like the pilot, as a developer, you will have a team to support you:

Planning consultant

Architect

Accountant

Solicitor

Commercial finance broker

Mentors

Insurance broker

Joint venture partner

Quantity surveyor

You will have a team to support you through the development stage:

Builder

Solicitor

Accountant

Mentors

And then a team to help complete the development:

Commercial finance broker

Insurance broker

Solicitor

Accountant

Mentors

Throughout the phases of development, there will be other experts who can step in to help you, such as warranty providers, structural engineers, and surveyors, but the ones listed above comprise the main power team that you will regularly rely upon.

Don't try to do all the work yourself. My partner and I don't attempt to design the buildings we want to build. We don't do the searches required to start the site. We don't create the planning applications and submit them to the local planning authorities. We don't search the markets for the best insurance provider or development finance lender. Tap the skills of the experts around you, who excel in what they do, to help you become a property developer.

What property development does require of you is to understand how the process works. This book is written to support you to become a developer, to believe in yourself and your vision. But the education part is also key.

Getting the education of developments is a bit like tackling a jigsaw puzzle. You start by opening the box and shaking out all of the pieces. Some may fall face up, revealing bits and pieces of what you already know about developments. You might know an architect. You might already know a solicitor. You may even know a builder. You, yourself, might already occupy the role of a power team member. Those pieces that lie face up represent what you know, so you don't need to do anything with them for now.

The pieces that are face down represent the components of a development project that are yet unfamiliar to you. Education is what turns the pieces over; it reveals to you the previously unknown parts of the puzzle so you can better understand them.

Once you have turned over all of the pieces, you can organise them and start to put the puzzle together. You collate your power team. Once you have a good understanding of the ins and outs of the development process, you are now ready for the practical part.

The practical part will have its challenges, and each project will be individual, with its own unique challenges, but education is about being prepared, knowing what to expect, what to anticipate, what to embrace and what to safeguard against, and how to deal with them.

Remember: The moment you quit is the moment you fail. Quitters never win, and winners never quit. You are a winner because you aren't afraid to get started.

Over the past few years I have understood the importance of having a team behind me. That's why they are called the power team. Together, you are a team. You are the captain. You are the leader. It is your role to organise the team. A well-structured team will find developments easier than a team that are unprepared.

Choosing the right team is essential. You want people with experience, who know what they are doing and who have done it before.

Let's look at some of the places and ways that you can find some of your power team. Based on my personal experience, one of the best ways to source a power team is through business network events.

BNI is a great source of power team members, and when I was part of that business network group for about a year, it included an accountant, an insurance broker, a builder, an electrician, a contracts writer, a plumber, a roofer, a safety equipment supplier, a carpet and flooring supplier, a branding expert, a web designer, a financial planner, a kitchen fitter, and a window supplier. All of these are useful in developments. It is a great way to find people to work with.

If you want a closer way to find more specific trades, then word of mouth recommendations will pay off. If you want to find a builder, have a walk around your local area and look for the development sites where the builders are doing what you want to build. If you are looking at building four or five houses, look for builders building four or five houses.

Visit your local builders merchants and ask for recommendations. They will probably give you the names of the builders who spend the most money with them as that's in their best interest, but it's also likely those same builders have a lot going on and are good at what they do.

We have also met some decent contacts at social events. These are not only fun but a great way to connect with people.

The most important thing to do when looking for power team members is to get out and be proactive, but at the end of the day, whoever you choose may not end up being your final power team member. We are on our third accountant, our second solicitor, and our third commercial mortgage broker, not because we didn't get on with the earlier ones, or because they did a bad job, but because we grew bigger than they could cope with.

We currently participate in three mentorship groups and have probably spent almost £80,000 on our own education since our initial investment back in 2014. The more we grow, the more we need education and support. We will always seek to have mentors. The power of knowledge from people who have been there and done that is invaluable. You can't put a true price on investing in yourself, but you can choose whether or not to make it pay.

Teamwork is the ability to work together toward a common vision. The ability to direct individual accomplishments toward organizational objectives. It is the fuel that allows common people to attain uncommon results. – Andrew Carnegie

Secret Tip #7: Search your local council's planning portal for planning applications that are consistently approved to identify the most skilled architects operating in your locale. Their business names appear on the bottom of every plan.

Chapter 6 Overcoming Obstacles

A common misconception of property development is that before you undertake it, you need to: a) be experienced; b) have money; and c) know what you're doing.

I would agree with the last point, that it's important to know what you're doing. Admittedly, Andi and I didn't meet a single one of these three requirements when we first started. We learnt by doing, as we went along, which is certainly not something, based on hindsight, that I would recommend now. We made the mistakes, but now we know what to look out for. It is better to fail trying than fail to start. You only truly fail when you stop trying.

Most people who are new to and interested in developments confess to me many of the same reasons as to why they are not developing property already. I'm sure you can relate to some of these:

Lack of money

Lack of free time

Lack of knowledge

Lack of confidence

Lack of an established track record

Risk

Fear

No power team in place

Mind-set

Self-doubt

Negs (the people who tell you that you can't do something. What they really mean is that they can't, or they're afraid to, so they try to dissuade you too)

All of these can be overcome. When we first started, I certainly didn't have any money. I didn't have time either. I only had sales knowledge and experience in selling new-build property, and that wasn't really valuable in that our goal wasn't to sell but to keep the properties.

I had no track record of developing, and I was taking on huge risks, which made me fearful. I had no power team apart from Andi, who only had a handful of people he had used before on some of his conversions and extension projects. Perhaps the only thing on that list that I had was a positive mind-set and the determination to succeed. I have always been a positive thinker, I love problem solving and a challenge, and I don't let anything get me down.

Think. What is stopping you getting started? The fact that you're reading this means you're interested. Money can be found, time can be leveraged, knowledge can be learnt, confidence can be gained, a track record can be borrowed, risk can be mitigated, fear can be reduced, a power team can be sourced, a mind-set can be changed, self-doubt can be squashed, and the negs can be ignored.

Nothing should stop you from starting. Remember, you don't have to be great to start. No one is an Olympic swimmer when they take their first plunge. It comes with practice. You can get great later. When babies learn to walk and they take a few tumbles in those first few weeks or months, do they give up? No. They carry on, they learn and they adapt, and the next time they make sure they have something to hold onto and to help themselves up. They are persistent and determined. Why should you be any different? If you want something badly enough, you will find only reasons to keep going; otherwise you only find excuses.

Is your reason for starting big enough? Don't wait for a reason similar to mine to get started. Property developments can lead to financial freedom. There are many benefits to property development. One thing for sure is that it's not easy. If it were, everyone would be doing it, because the rewards can be life-changing. It takes a lot to do a development, including patience.

This book has been designed and written to show you that we started and we learnt along the way – and now we teach others how to start. Property developments have unquestionably changed my life for the better. They have certainly changed my family's lives, and for that I am forever thankful for having started.

I now drive a car that I dreamt about for year, because I believed in myself. I live in a nice property with my amazing family because I have worked for it. Some people only see the swan gliding along the water looking peaceful. Some of what Andi and I have achieved has been hard, it's been tough and people don't see the swan's feet frantically paddling beneath the surface to keep moving forward.

We keep going. We learn from our mistakes and we get better each time. And now we make sure that you don't make the mistakes that we made.

What reason would inspire you to start? What do you want in your life that you haven't got already? What dreams have you had that are yet unfulfilled? Just for a moment, after reading this, take a minute to reflect, picture your dream car on the drive of your dream house. Your family are ready to go away on that dream holiday you have always envisioned. The charity that you support have just thanked you for your very generous donation.

Picture a significant amount of money that would help you, your family, and your dreams – what is it? What is stopping you from achieving earning that amount? Why haven't you started already?

It feels good. So what are you waiting for? Start today. Make it happen. Stop dreaming of the life that you'd love and start living the life that you dream.

I'm not saying that everybody should go out and start property developing. It is not for everyone. What I want to share is that anyone can do it if they really want to. You have to want to.

It is a challenging business. It has its ups and downs. Every business enterprise does. We've been through many, and I will share them with you throughout this book. It can be a business if you want it to be, but it can also be a side-line if you prefer – a hobby.

The 10 primary parts to property development, based on our experience, are:

1. You can never do too much due diligence

2. Having the right team around you is key

3. Expect problems along the way; how you manage them is what's important, not how well you tried to ignore that they might happen

4. Always overestimate your build costs

5. Be realistic when calculating your expected gross development value (GDV)

6. Establish a plan A, a Plan B, and a Plan C (the 'Armageddon' plan) as exit strategies.

7. Understand the health and safety aspects of a development and comply with the rules and regulations, especially the Construction Design and Management 2015 Act, as the consequences of not doing so can be costly

8. Comprehend the process you are undertaking and what is realistically involved

9. Buy at the right price and keep an eye on the budget, not just in purchasing the plot but later costs, the materials, fees, etc. (if you take charge of that), start to finish

10. Just do it - get started by getting educated, and then do, by following the process of people who have done it in the past

(You can ignore all of the above if you prefer to just sit back and do nothing.)

Although property development comes with its share of challenges, the rewards at the end of a project are worth it, believe me. Those rewards are not just money related, although most people think of property development primarily as a way to make a load of money. That is true in some respects but it all depends on how you purchase the site and what you do with it.

Rewards from property development are as much a feeling of personal achievement as making money. And, in terms of the money you can make from property development, it's what you do with the property that's more important.

Let's look at a fictional property development deal that makes an after-tax profit of £400,000. That may sound like a lot of money to you, or it might not. (That's another thing about this taboo word, money. Everyone sees it in a different light. Good or bad, some people love it whilst others profess to despise it; some dream of it and others wish they didn't have quite so much. Remember, it's not that money is the root of all evil; it's the love of money that's the root of all evil. Money is just money. And what you do with your money is up to you. A few book recommendations on the psychology of money include Mind over Money, by Claudia Hammond, and Money, by Rob Moore.)

Okay, so you've just made £400,000. Picture it for a moment. Picture yourself walking down the road to your local cash machine. There's a queue of people in front of you to use the machine, but once they finish, you find yourself standing in front on it, looking at the screen.

You insert your card. It's one of those machines that seem to take your card very slowly. You punch in your PIN and hesitate. Rather than press the button that everyone else presses, Cash, no receipt, your finger hovers over another one. It's the one that anxious teenagers press: Show balance on screen. You press it.

Yesterday it showed £1.27 in your account. Today? Your balance is £400,001.27.

What would you do? What might you do? Would this available cash change your life? Whose life could you change with this figure? Could you buy that dream car you've always wanted? (For me, this month it's the Ferrari 488 GTB, but it will probably be different next month.)

Where could you go on holiday? What other plots could you put your money towards? Does early retirement beckon?

All of these are possible simply because you made more money. It is a taboo thing to discuss in polite society for some reason, but not a day goes by without us hearing the word, or thinking about it, consciously or unconsciously. With money comes choice, and potentially freedom. It is probably a case of freedom of choice versus freedom to do what you want. When you have money, you have fewer limitations. You can do what you have always wanted, you can help those that you have always wanted to help, you can go where you want to go, and drive the car you have always wanted.

The feeling I get when driving past one of our developments, knowing that we built it, we created it, we gave our tenants a home, we paid our contractors for their time and effort, we helped the council and the Government with their housing requirements, we helped to regenerate the town, we did something that challenged us and we succeeded – it's nothing short of exhilarating.

All of these are internal feelings. Feelings that make you smile, feelings that have a positive effect on others. If we can achieve that every time we build new properties, how amazing is that?

Along with the ego drive of creating new properties, the money that has come from property development has changed my family's life. Two thousand fourteen was a huge year for me. I committed to starting a new business, I purchased a plot of land with my partner Andi, I got married (to my other partner, Lydia, not Andi! ha ha), I left my day job to devote myself to the new business full-time, and one of the biggest changes for Lydia and me was when we found out we were expecting our first child. Lydia has been a tremendous support for me since deciding to start our business. In fact, a lot of my family members have been influential in helping me and our business grow. My mum, stepdad, mother-in-law, and my nan were, and still are, superb in helping us.

Lydia believed in me from the start. I worried about telling her initially in 2014 that Andi and I wanted to commit to a 12-month mentorship programme. It was a cost I couldn't cover and I had no money. I had never even taken a credit card out before, as I saw them as a rabbit hole. But I had the determination and desire to do what I had always dreamt of, and knew that in order to succeed I had to do something different.

I paid for the mentorship on a 0% interest credit card and made the minimum payments each month, because that was all I could afford to do at the time. Lydia did worry about my spending so much on something new, and all but unknown, but I reassured her time and time again that I would do whatever it took to make it profitable. Her ability to trust me helped, as we have managed to change our lives.

At the time, Lydia was working as a nurse at a private hospital chain. She enjoyed it, but it was long hours. She would leave at 6:00 a.m. and not return home until 19:30 or 20:00. Needless to say, I didn't get to see her much on those days. My mum also had reservations, not because she didn't have faith in me but more because she knew I tended to start something and get bored halfway through and abandon it. She didn't want to see that happen again, especially with so much at stake, but the difference this time was that I had changed my mind-set. I had a reason to succeed. I had a why.

A why is a reason to do something. A why is the reason you get out of bed every morning – it is the reason you do what you do. You do it for a purpose. My why in 2014 was to start a business, prove to myself and my family that I could be successful, and take the first steps to create a life of choice – my choice. And each year since, my why has changed.

In 2014, I started the business and left my day job, determined to make a new life for Lydia and me and make my dad and grandad proud that I have started something that I had always dreamt of starting.

In 2015, our first child, Arlo, was born, and he added to my why. I had always wanted a boy and was delighted. He is awesome.

In 2016, my previous whys continued to expand, this time to include the arrival of our second child, Albie. I continued to do property developments for my family. I continued to improve daily, to improve not only myself but also our future, eager to leave a legacy for my family.

In 2017, I looked at my values and what I truly enjoy, and that's travelling. I did it when I left school in 2005 and I want to continue to travel, and maybe stemming from my earlier obsession with flags of the world, I have now set a goal to travel to pretty much every country in the world. I love travelling. And property is the vehicle that enables me to live my dreams and realise my ambitions.

Another thing I want is for my children to have choices when they grow up. I want to teach them the value of money and how it can be used to create the lifestyle they desire. I want to be a mentor to my children and leave a legacy that can be passed down from generation to generation. (Perhaps there will someday hang an oil painting of me, Rockefeller style, in my great-great-great-great-grandchild's house. Haha.)

If my children decide that they want to get into property, then I will support them and potentially pass down my share of our portfolio at the time. The majority of our properties are on interest-only repayment mortgages, so they can assume my debt. I'm kind like that.

The Grosvenor Estate is a classic example of this theory of passing down property and debt through generations. It has assets of roughly $59.5 billion, accumulated from doing business since 1677. The Grosvenor Estate own parts of London, like Mayfair and Belgravia, which, in 1677, comprised swamps, pastures, and orchards. This is the compound effect. Since the 1600s, property has always increased in value over time. It has peaks and troughs, but over time it increases. This is why we adopt the build-to-rent strategy. It is a wealth-building strategy. My advice to you is to start doing what you have always wanted to do and create the future that you have always dreamt of.

Secret Tip #8: Create a vision board. A vision board is like a dream board. Add pictures of everything you would like to achieve in your life. Keep it visible and on display. The law of attraction will make those dreams reality. Make sure you think about them as you work towards achieving your dreams. My vision board is becoming my reality board.

Chapter 7 The Planning Process

There are some important parts to a good development site. The better you can prepare yourself at the beginning, the easier it will be throughout the process. The planning process of a development is fundamental to a development's success.

Every new-build development site requires a permission to build. This is the planning permission. Every council has a need to build more houses, as set out by the UK Government in the National Planning Policy Framework.[5] Rt Hon Greg Clark MP was the Minister of Planning in 2012, and the foreword included in the National Planning Policy Framework from him states:

The purpose of planning is to help achieve sustainable development.

Sustainable means ensuring that better lives for ourselves don't [sic] mean worse lives for future generations.

Development means growth. We must accommodate the new ways by which we will earn our living in a competitive world. We must house a rising population, which is living longer and wants to make new choices. We must respond to the changes that new technologies offer us. Our lives, and the places in which we live them, can be better, but they will certainly be worse if things stagnate.

Sustainable development is about change for the better, and not only in our built environment.

Our natural environment is essential to our wellbeing, and it

5   This excerpt consists of public sector information licensed under the Open Government Licence v3.0. See https://www.gov.uk/government/uploads/system/uploads/attachment_data/file/6077/2116950.pdf.

can be better looked after than it has been. Habitats that have been degraded can be restored. Species that have been isolated can be reconnected. Green Belt land that has been depleted of diversity can be refilled by nature – and opened to people to experience it, to the benefit of body and soul.

Our historic environment – buildings, landscapes, towns and villages – can better be cherished if their spirit of place thrives, rather than withers.

Our standards of design can be so much higher. We are a nation renowned worldwide for creative excellence, yet, at home, confidence in development itself has been eroded by the too frequent experience of mediocrity.

So sustainable development is about positive growth – making economic, environmental and social progress for this and future generations.

The planning system is about helping to make this happen.

Development that is sustainable should go ahead, without delay – a presumption in favour of sustainable development that is the basis for every plan, and every decision. This framework sets out clearly what could make a proposed plan or development unsustainable.

In order to fulfil its purpose of helping achieve sustainable development, planning must not simply be about scrutiny. Planning must be a creative exercise in finding ways to enhance and improve the places in which we live our lives.

This should be a collective enterprise. Yet, in recent years, planning has tended to exclude, rather than to include, people and communities. In part, this has been a result of targets being imposed, and decisions taken, by bodies remote from *them. Dismantling the unaccountable regional apparatus and introducing neighbourhood planning addresses this.*

In part, people have been put off from getting involved because planning policy itself has become so elaborate and forbidding – the preserve of specialists, rather than people in communities.

This National Planning Policy Framework changes that. By replacing over a thousand pages of national policy with around fifty, written simply and clearly, we are allowing people and communities back into planning.

He makes some very valid points in the statement, and ones we can use to help us obtain planning permission. The National Planning Practice Guidance,[6] which is regularly updated, sets out how the National Planning Policy Framework is applied.

When you apply for planning permission, there are many aspects to consider and rules to adhere to. Each council has its own local policy, which can fall under any number of names; for example, the council's development plan, policy plan, development proposal, local plan, local development framework, etc. – different names for the same thing. The local policy sets out what each council requires. A simple planning application should be policy compliant and give the council exactly what they require. Contrary to belief, the planning officers in the council are there to grant planning, not refuse it. If your application aligns to their local policy, the officers are more likely to grant permission.

When looking at a potential development site, there are lots of things to consider, including but not limited to:

• What potential constraints are there?

---

6   See https://www.gov.uk/government/collections/planning-practice-guidance.

- What does the local policy require?

- Is the land suitable for development?

- Is there a demand for houses?

- What contributions would I need to consider, and how much?

One way to ensure you don't have to go through the planning process is to acquire a development site with planning permission already granted. This mitigates the uncertainty associated with purchasing a site without planning. Finding the right site takes patience and an understanding of what to look for. It is also important to know that, having said that, even sites with planning are not always the best choice. While it can be advantageous to be able to mitigate the risk of being denied planning, some sites with planning have a load of hoops to jump through before you can commence work, conditions on the planning permission that must be met. On a fairly straightforward permission I would expect to see about four to eight conditions, but I have seen planning permissions granted with more than forty conditions attached. Conditions come in three 'flavours':

- Pre-commencement (conditions or work you must carry out before any works start onsite)

- Pre-occupation (conditions that must be discharged before first occupation)

- Performance (Conditions that must be dealt with throughout the development)

Sites without planning require you to file a planning application before making any improvements.

Planning, or planning permission, is the process imposed by

the 1947 Town and Country Planning Act which established that planning permission is required for land development; ownership alone no longer confers the right to develop the land. The Act reorganised the planning system, reducing it from 1,400 planning authorities to 145 (formed from county and borough councils), and requires each to prepare a comprehensive development plan. A planning permission is now required for all new developments as outlined in Section 55 (1) of the 1990 Town and Country Planning Act.

Andi and I utilise our planning consultant, a member of our power team, to do the hard work for us. I say 'hard' because Andi and I don't know the ins and outs of the planning system. That is the role our power team plays. Our planning consultant, Jonathon McDermott from TPX Planning, or 'Harry Potter's fatter cousin' as he refers to himself, is amazing at what he does. He knows the Town and Country Planning Act inside out and could recite it in his sleep.

When submitting a planning application, some of the key aspects need to consider the following:

- Planning policy

- The principle of development of the site

- The development's design/appearance

- The effect of the development on adjoining or surrounding properties

- Its effect on the safety and convenience of the highway

- Site-specific planning considerations (heritage, flooding, noise, etc.)

- Planning obligations and CIL (community infrastructure levy)

All decisions are planning policy led and must relate back to a specific set of policies.

Let's say you can do a quick viability of your site by looking at the surrounding area. Most local planning officers like consistency, so look around. What is the character of the street? What adjoins the site? How tall are the buildings adjoining and adjacent to the site? To what scale are they?

Ensuring your suggested development is in keeping with the surrounding area will give you more traction in getting planning. Character is king.

Other factors to consider when looking at a property development site include whether planning application was submitted previously and, if so, the outcome. If the site had planning permission that has since lapsed – permissions last for three years, unless otherwise stated – what was granted? Can you reinstate the old permission? It's not always certain that you will be granted planning permission again, but it is probably more of a likelihood than a site that has never been granted planning permission.

Has the site had refused planning? If so, refusals come with reasons. Can you alter the reasons for refusal to create a plan that conforms to policy?

Is the site in open countryside? If so, this may fall out of what is called the 'greenbelt'. The greenbelt is an entirely different designation from greenfield land in that its preservation is given legal status. In general, no new development is allowed on greenbelt land, unless it fits in with Government requirements. If you do want to build in the countryside – even on greenbelt – it can be done under paragraph 55 of the National Planning Policy

- Framework. It is not straightforward, but neither is it impossible.

Once you have assessed the site for its viability and decided what you would like to build, it's time to look at different ways to maximize the site's full potential. By that I mean to work out what property type and size works best for maximum profit. The minimum size standards for new-build development indicate the smallest property you are permitted to develop. If this is your strategy, that's fine, as cramming as many units into the site as possible isn't always the best option. For example, ten 2-bed houses squeezed onto a site may only have a gross development value of £1.5 million, whereas a site with six 4-bed houses may be valued at £1.8 million and cost about the same to build. It's important to take time to work out the best solutions for the site, as it can make or break your project.

Table 1 - Minimum gross internal floor areas and storage (m^2)

Number of bedrooms(b)	Number of bed spaces (persons)	1 storey dwellings	2 storey dwellings	3 storey dwellings	Built-in storage
	1p	39 (37) *			1.0
1b	2p	50	58		1.5
	3p	61	70		
2b	4p	70	79		2.0
	4p	74	84	90	
3b	5p	86	93	99	2.5
	6p	95	102	108	
	5p	90	97	103	
	6p	99	106	112	
4b	7p	108	115	121	3.0
	8p	117	124	130	
	6p	103	110	116	
5b	7p	112	119	125	3.5
	8p	121	128	134	
	7p	116	123	129	
6b	8p	125	132	138	4.0

Section 106 of the Town and Planning Act

During a planning application, the site may be subject to Section 106 of the Town and Planning Act, which allows for local planning authorities to request contributions, arrangements, and restrictions to help towards the provision of new amenities and those roads directly affected by the increase in the number of houses within the area of development. These are generally monetary contributions.

As developers, this is something that can be negotiated using a viability assessment to demonstrate that the development would not be otherwise viable were the contributions taken. This includes CIL (community infrastructure levy) and Affordable Housing. Typically, the viability threshold is 20% over the capital cost of the development, and not the GDV.

In a recent case at the High Court in 2015, between West Berkshire District Council and Reading Borough Council versus Secretary of State for Communities and Local Government, it was decided that developments with no more than 10 houses with an aggregate (combined) gross floor area of no more than 1,000 square metres would be exempt from Section 106. Affordable houses will come into play when the site exceeds the above, but, again, this can be negotiated with a viability study. If you are unsure, always check with the local council or, better still, your planning consultant. One way to mitigate the uncertainty of Section 106 payments is to stick to development sites of no more than 10 houses where the gross floor area does not exceed 1,000 square metres. There are plenty of sites available that suit this kind of size development.

Affordable Housing is a part of Section 106 and, as such, also exempts those developments with no more than 10 houses and a maximum gross floor area of 1,000 square metres. Affordable houses are new housing developments that are offered at a fraction of the original cost to people who cannot afford main market housing.

The different types of affordable houses are:

- affordable (social) rent

- affordable (social) sale

- intermediate social rent or sale

Affordable housing is offered to the housing provider at an established cost ration, meaning it's discounted from the market value, depending on the council and/or housing authority. Typically, you take little or no profit from an affordable house. This will need to be factored into your appraisals when looking at larger developments.

Community Infrastructure Levy (CIL) is the newer way of taking planning contributions and is based on a flat rate of a certain price per square metre of new development. For example, in Northampton, the council have adopted around £50 per square metre. Other areas may be higher or lower. The highest I have seen is £495 per square metre. Not having that information could really affect your site development.

To make the most out of your development, we recommend implementing a planning consultant at the very start of your development strategy and appraisal phase. Have the planning consultant on the project all the way through the planning process and allow them to instruct the architects and other team members.

With developments, we always look to mitigate the risks as much as possible, something we incorporate in the planning stage. One of the biggest risks is not getting planning, and ways to mitigate this include having a fall-back position, an alternative to the scheme you submit that is more likely to get planning. This fall-back position is what you should always base your purchase offer on, not your most potentially profitable scenario.

Another way to mitigate not getting planning would be to follow a policy-compliant strategy, where you stick strictly to the local development plan the whole way through the development. Remember, their goal is to grant you planning, whenever possible, so by sticking to what the council says they want, why would they not give you planning? Any refusal has to be based on non-adherence; they can't just refuse planning arbitrarily if your proposal adheres to their policies – that is, just because they got out of the wrong side of the bed that morning.

During the planning process, there are different types of planning applications. Each one is used for different reasons. Let's look at the various types of applications.

Pre-application (pre-app)

A pre-application enquiry is a pre-assessment of a planning permission by the Local Planning Authority (the planning department) and its consultees. It is submitted to the planning department of the council and assessed in accordance with the council's own criteria.

There are no standard charges for a pre-app – each council is allowed to set its own fees, and there are no statutory time limits; however, most attempt to answer within 21 days.

A pre-application is a good process to use for an initial consultation as it can save you time and money, help you to understand the local authority's development plan, identify potential problems early on, and help you to solve them, as well as help you obtain the best advice on your scheme before submitting a full application.

The more you can provide the local authority at this stage, the better. It gives them a more comprehensive understanding of the scheme so they can give you the most suitable advice. The local authority should give you positive advice to help improve your scheme.

The pre-application is generally confidential, and you are permitted to submit them on sites you don't currently own, meaning the owner would be unaware of your application. Some councils do release their pre-application advice once a related further application is submitted, making the pre-application advice public at that point. This is a good way to determine whether or not a site would be viable. It is important to know that the pre-application is not legally binding and is based on one planner's thoughts and not that of the council's policy.

Prior notification/prior approval

Prior notification applications are required as a condition of permitted development rights, and form a simplified application which the Council has for a fixed period, typically 56 days.

The criteria on which they are assessed is set out within the General Permitted Development Order(s), the most recent at the time of this writing being the 2015 order, which was amended in 2017.

Most prior notification applications have a standing fee of £96 where no building works are required, or £206 where building works are required. These are only for change-of-use applications and do not apply to new-build developments.

Outline planning

Outline planning permissions are often used by speculative developers to allow the assessment of some (but generally not all) of the material considerations in a planning application. These material considerations are:

- Scale

- Layout

- Access

- Appearance

- Landscape

Applicants have the principle of development assessed, and any of the reserved matters, or material considerations, i.e., the scale, layout, access, appearance, and landscape.

The outline application usually takes the same amount of time as full applications, generally eight weeks for minor developments (1–9 units inclusive) and 13 weeks for major developments (10–199 units inclusive).

The benefit of an outline application are the lower fees associated with this kind of application. It is £462 per 0.1 hectare for sites up to and including 2.5 hectares. For bigger sites, those over 2.5 hectares, the price is £11,432 + £138 per 0.1 hectare, with a maximum cost of £150,000.

An outline planning application is not allowed for conversions or changes of use. They are only available for new developments.

Reserved matters

Reserved matters applications are a form of 'discharge of condition application' where the reserved matters not assessed in the outline are brought for assessment.

Reserved matters applications take the same time as full applications and carry the same fee as full application, £462 per dwelling. The timescales are the same as a full application, generally eight weeks for minor developments (1–9 units inclusive) and 13 weeks for major developments (10–199 units inclusive).

The council extracts the full fee on this type of application.

Full planning

Full planning permission (or simply planning permission) is a formal application to the planning authority where all of the determining issues are assessed in full.

The time periods and the fees involved for a full planning permission are the same as above, £462 per dwelling and eight weeks for minor developments (1–9 units inclusive) and 13 weeks for major developments (10–199 units inclusive). On some occasions the council may ask for an extension of time.

Developments that consist of 200 or more houses are considered strategic developments. Councils tend to like strategic developments, as they meet a large proportion of the required units within their policy.

There are six steps to a full planning application. These steps, or stages, are largely governed by legislation.

Step 1 – Validation

The applications are first checked for omissions. Depending on your council, this normally takes around three working days. The checks make sure all the required documents and fees have been submitted, and in the correct manner.

Step 2 – Consultation and publicity

The consultation period, usually 21 days from the date of publishing, is the period open for discussion with local, neighbouring residents to the site. The application is also advertised in local papers, appropriate local websites, and on lampposts near the proposed site. Various bodies who might be affected by the site are also consulted, such as the Highways Authority, parish councils, environmental agencies, etc.

When the consultation period is open, neighbouring residents can add their opinion to the applications. Ninety-nine times out of one hundred, this will be an objection to, rather than support of, the site, as those who are not opposed to it likely feel no need to weigh in. Some of the comments will be valid; others may be nonsensical, most stemming from the NIMBY (not in my back yard) mind-set. People, by nature, resist change, however, and so generally, initially, they will object to new developments, even though they might generate a positive impact on their property, and increase its value, such as through gentrification.

In one instance, two brothers who were my students put in an application for a development of two flats – nothing huge. A neighbour objected, submitting several letters outlining his objections, which included:

By building upwards with an extra floor, my view of the green fields will be blocked. Less sunlight will cover my garden and increase the damp and slippery moss, which builds up on my back garden pathway.

These issues will no doubt affect my current good neighbours to some similar degree too, affecting our quality of life and safety. Slipping on moss is not something I would wish on anybody. It's a drain on the NHS and Ambulance Service too.

Some of the objections are not planning reasons, and are often dismissed accordingly, but they do make for entertaining reading. Other written objections I've seen include:

I used to have the nicest house on the street and now I won't, so stop it.

There are too many new houses in the street. It doesn't look like when I bought here in 1968.

They will use the retail shops. The shops are becoming too crowded.

They will be able to look over the fence at my dog.

It may be worth knocking on your site neighbour's door to advise them of your planning application prior to submission in case you can stave off objections before they write to the council. We have offered solutions such as to fix a fence whilst the builders are onsite, if desired. Any goodwill you can create in advance can only help the situation.

Step 3 – Consideration

The site's planning case officer will inspect the site and the application, and assess the local authority's planning policies, consultation responses, and public representations.

Step 4 – Negotiation

If problems are identified with the application, which there is scope to address through alterations to the proposal, the officer will contact the applicant to seek suitable amendments. Steps 2 and 3 may require to be repeated, if amendments made significantly change the application.

Step 5 – Recommendation

The planning officer will make a recommendation via the officers' report on the application to the person or relevant council committee authorised to make a decision.

There may be occasions when an application is referred to an Area Planning Committee for a decision, such as when a Division Member has carefully assessed the merits of the application and decided sufficient planning reasons exist for it to be determined by the committee. If the application is decided by delegated decision, this will be via the Principal Planning Officer, who signs the planning permission.

Ninety per cent of all planning applications are decided by the delegated route. If the application is to be decided at a committee meeting, objectors and the applicant are advised of the time and venue of the meeting. All meetings are public and all interested parties are free to attend and observe how a decision is reached.

Step 6 – Decision

A decision is taken on the application by the appropriate body.

With most householder applications the Director of Planning normally makes the decision under what's known as 'delegated powers'. This means that they can make the decision without going to the relevant committee, which speeds up the process. Around 90% of householder applications are decided this way.

Where the decision lies with a committee, that committee may perform a site inspection. In reaching a decision, the committee is required by law to limit the matters it takes into account to the 'Development Plan', i.e., the Structure Plan and Local Plan policies relating to the application and to other planning matters, often referred to as material considerations. What does and does not qualify as a planning matter varies between applications but can generally be summarised as the impact of the proposed development on the surrounding environment and infrastructure. Matters which should not be taken into account include the identity of the person applying, their past history, and any potential effect on the value of neighbouring properties.

The application must, under the legislation, be determined in accordance with the Development Plan, unless other matters indicate that this is inappropriate. It is therefore useful to be aware of the content of the Development Plan prior to submitting an application.

This information on these six steps appears on the Wiltshire Council website, which explains the process very well.[7]

Discharge of conditions

This is submitted after planning permission is granted to address any condition that requires further details. Conditions are imposed to overcome a harmful effect of the development.

The fee for a discharge of condition is £95 per request and not per condition (many conditions can be included in one request) and they take a fixed time period of eight weeks, after which you enjoy deemed consent.

Appeal

Appeals to the Secretary of State may be made following refusals of planning permission where a resubmission is not an option. Appeals are made directly to the Planning Inspectorate.

There is no charge for an appeal, as it is included in the original planning fee. Note though that appeals presently take up to five months to complete).

All property developments require a full application to be granted and all pre-commencement conditions to be discharged before you may start improvements on the site. Once a full planning application has been granted, unless it states otherwise, the

7   See http://www.wiltshire.gov.uk/planninganddevelopment/householdersguidetoplanning/theplanningprocess.htm.

permission remains valid for three years. The planning permission is attached to the land, so this can be sold on with the land, a strategy known as planning gain. The value of land is increased with planning gain and so can be sold on, generally for a profit.

We shape our buildings; thereafter, they shape us. –Winston Churchill

Secret Tip #9: Decide with your planning consultant the best application to submit, keeping in mind the end user. If you build to rent, consider 2–3-beds as opposed to 4–5-beds, and assess the price of the properties against the build costs to gain maximum efficiency.

Chapter 8 How to Find a Development Site

One of the biggest barriers stopping people from starting property developments is their confidence in finding suitable land, or land in general. It might be that they have low self-belief in what they can achieve, or it might be that they believe in themselves but think there are no deals out there. Whatever their reasons, I can assure you that there are development plots out there. Eighty-nine per cent of England hasn't been built on, and there were 27.1 million households in the UK in 2016, according to the Office for National Statistics. Land is available and the Government need houses.

Let's look at where to focus your search initially to make it easier to find land with development potential. There are two main types of development plots to look for, greenfield and brownfield. It is not the colour of the grass or earth that defines the two; it is the nature of the land. Brownfield developments are plots of land that had previous planning use but which may have since ceased, such as former factories, builders yards, and disused petrol stations, to name but a few examples, while greenfield denotes land that has never been commercially developed.

St James in Northampton, our first purchase at auction, was a brownfield site, having consisted of 22 garages, whilst a site we developed of 11 houses was situated on a fire-damaged factory site. In fact, almost all of our development sites are brownfield sites. Local planning authorities are keen for the redevelopment of brownfield sites over greenfield sites for a number of reasons, in essence having them recycled. Vacant sites may be valuable, but when not utilised, are generally viewed as blemishing the landscape, which councils don't want.

Brownfield sites generally lie within an already established developed area. It may be in or close to residential areas too, which helps. There is no need for people to commute to the town or city if you can develop within it, which also serves to reduce traffic congestion and pollution, in looking at the bigger picture.

Redevelopment of a brownfield site also promotes gentrification, which has a positive effect on the nearby properties by eradicating an eyesore, which can boost house prices. If a new three-bed house of a similar size to those around it is valued higher, then the overall street value starts to rise.

Although there are many positive reasons for brownfield site redevelopment, there are some precautions which should be taken. When a previous use existed on the site, the ground should always be tested for contamination, as the cost of remedial work required to remove any contaminated land will increase your costs.

The site may require demolition of an existing building, which must be factored into your development costs. There might be underlying pipework that could be hard or expensive to move and prevent you from building on or around it.

One advantage to brownfield sites is that they typically feature existing services like electricity, water, and/or gas, which you may be able to exploit for your development.

Greenfield sites, again, are plots that have not previously been developed, generally agricultural or natural areas left to evolve. Because the land has not been developed previously, there is nothing to demolish and there tends to be no existing issues, minimising those types of costs. Greenfield land is most often located on the outskirts of towns or cities, although you do get the occasional sites within a town and city, but councils generally prefer to maintain any green space within an urban area, making it harder to obtain planning permission as it may fall out of the council's local proposed development plans.

The council's local proposed development plan (your council may call it something similar) covers future development of the local area. It is created by the local planning authority in consultation with the community, under the Planning and Compulsory Purchase Act 2004. You can find your local proposed development plan by searching your council website, usually under the planning section, sometimes under a heading like 'Planning for the future'.

Viewing such a plan is useful as it illustrates where the local planning authority desire residential development. If you can find a plot of land within the highlighted area, you are more likely to be granted planning permission for a residential development on it. Other factors would still need to be approved on the planning application, but the council will be more predisposed to accept the application.

Once you have looked at the local proposed development plan, you are ready to start your search for development plots. I always recommend you start your search in a town or city that you know, one that is local (easily accessible) to you. We call this the goldmine area. Your goldmine area's sites are not only convenient to you but your local knowledge is also priceless when it comes to understanding the demographics of the people likely to live in the properties. You wouldn't build a high-end, luxury, six-bed, 5,000-square-foot mansion next to a council estate, or vice-versa. Choose an area you know, that's near you, and know what you are building. Having the right property, one that suits the area, is essential.

9 ways to find a development site

There are nine key ways we use to find a development site. The more of these you employ, the more likely you are to find a development site. .

- Websites

- Agents

- Word of mouth

- Getting out and about (visits to the neighbourhoods)

- Google Earth/Land Registry/Land Insight

- Councils

- Auctions

- Deal sourcers

- Power team members

Websites

A simple web search for 'land for sale' brings up sites like rightmove.co.uk, zoopla.co.uk, uklandandfarms.co.uk, primelocation.com, onthemarket.com, gumtree.com, and more. You want to use all of these websites. Many people only search one site, like Rightmove, and ignore the rest. We found a recent property on Zoopla that was not listed on Rightmove, so how many opportunities might we miss if we weren't thorough enough to search all of the appropriate websites?

You don't have to spend hours trawling through every page of every site. A quick search on Rightmove commercial, as I write this, for development opportunities in Northampton and the surrounding 40 miles generated a list of no fewer than 2,015 development opportunities, of which 977 were land development opportunities. There are loads of opportunities on the Internet. The challenge is that everyone else is looking on the same sites. You are competing with lots of other people who are already doing property development or have read this book in anticipation of starting their first project. And competition drives prices up. That said, although we use all nine key methods to find property, the vast majority of the deals Andi and I have done have been listed online at some point, so there are deals to be found, and searching the internet is one of the easier, more convenient ways to find property development sites.

Just don't let it be your only method.

Agents

Commercial agents are the usual source to find property development opportunities. Unlike residential agents, commercial agents specialise in land development opportunities, along with commercial offices, shops, and industrial and other investment properties. Start there, but don't dismiss residential agents, as they do have the odd land development site now and again, although you will probably find those listings online as well. You may find that you will have to chase commercial agents a bit more than residential agents.

One technique which will always serve you better than just a phone call is to visit your commercial agents, face to face, in their office. A face-to-face introduction will invariably make agents feel more receptive to you versus a disembodied voice over the phone. We naturally engage more fully with people when talking in person. Body language is powerful in meetings. Be memorable and be persistent.

Word of mouth

Tell as many people as you know that you are looking for land development opportunities, as this is one way to find off-market opportunities, ones that aren't advertised, that aren't on the internet, and therefore ones that agents don't know about.

You might have an opportunity to deal directly with the owner of the site, which can be a real advantage – less competition and an improved chance to negotiate a good deal for both you and the owner. Remember, the owner has to pay fees to agents too, so you could be saving them the fee.

We are not out to exploit sellers in order to get the cheapest possible property deals. We prefer deals where everyone involved is satisfied, from the seller to any agent involved, as well as us.

Out and about

Have you ever noticed that when you buy a new car, you suddenly see that same model car on the road more frequently? You didn't notice them so much, if at all, beforehand. This is because your brain is now consciously more aware of your model of car.

It's the same with land. When you are actively looking for land, you notice suitable plots far more frequently. When you know what you're looking for, it's easier to find. So, when you are out and about, whether it be driving around, walking the dog, running, cycling, or whatever floats your boat, keep one eye out for plots of land. Note where you saw each plot, or its GPS coordinates if possible, so you can investigate its potential. Once you know the location of the plot, you can use our favourite online technique to identify the owner, so you can contact them directly.

Google Maps/Land Registry/LandInsight

Imagine sitting on a sun lounger, surrounded by white sandy beaches. The sun is shining overhead, there is a gentle breeze, and the only sound you hear is that of waves lapping the shore. All this while you're looking for land. You might find a plot of land that would justify being on that sun lounger. By using Google Maps, you can skim locations for potential sites.

How? Click on the satellite bird's-eye view. Start in the centre of whatever town or city you're searching and look for patches of land in and around residential areas. You might need to zoom in and out to see them. Again, if you're familiar with the area, you will have the added benefit of knowing what you are looking at. This technique enables you to look at places that you might not normally venture past, and to see opportunities not easily spotted when simply driving or walking by. There may be some plots set back from the roadside, such as garden plots.

Remember to follow your local proposals map to look for those areas where the council indicates they need sites. It is also an advantage to look in residential areas. One thing to look for on the satellite view is anomalies, things that stand out and look odd within residential streets. That might be a set of garages, similar to our St James site. It might be a factory located in what is now the middle of a residential area. Councils are often anxious to relocate factories and industries to the more industrial parts of town.

Once you have identified a few plots, Google Maps lets you measure them. In the satellite (bird's-eye) view, right-click your mouse and select measure distance. Click your curser on the screen to indicate where you want to measure from and then click again where you want to measure to. This gives you a fairly accurate linear distance from one side of the site to the other.

This is also particularly useful for doing a preliminary assessment of buildable possibilities. For example, if the site were 50 metres wide, you can measure nearby residential properties to 50 metres. If, say, it's a row of terraced houses, there might be ten houses that fit within 50 metres, telling you that, subject to other factors, you could potentially fit ten houses on the site.

When you have your sites identified, log onto the Government land registry website, https://www.gov.uk/government/organisations/land-registry. Click Search property ownership information and then on the green Start now button, it will take you to the Government's main land registry site, which features a public database of land ownership.

Finding property is easy here, as you can type in the house name or number and the postcode and usually find the property details. It is harder to find empty land plots as there is no associated name or number and you may not know the postcode.

This is where the previous Google Maps search helps. By using its Map enquiry, you can locate plots from the land registry's home page. Enter your town or city into the search field and click Search to bring up the ordnance survey map of your town. Click Ordnance survey map and, on the drop-down menu, click on Bird's eye. Un-tick (de-select) Show angled view.

Now, use this map to locate your plot and zoom in. Once you have zoomed close enough to the site, click on the Find properties tab on the bottom left-hand side of the map. When it turns blue, click On and a white circle with an orange outline will appear. Position that circle inside the plot you are looking at and click on it. Scroll down and you should get the plot information. There will be three options: Title Register (£3), Title Plan (£3) and Flood Risk Indicator Result (£9).

Do not buy the Flood Risk Indicator Result!

Highlight the Title Register and Title Plan and purchase these for a total of £6. Wouldn't you pay £6 to potentially find a deal that might profit you far more? It might be a numbers game, but the more you can afford to do, the better. On the Title Register you will see the name and address of the owner(s), and often the original purchase price, and whether a lender is involved. Using this information, you can send the owner(s) a letter requesting to arrange a meeting with them to discuss a potential purchase.

The Title Register is a great tool for negotiation too. it often reveals how much they paid for the land and whether it was a recent purchase or they have sat on it for a while. If they have had it awhile, the value may have increased, although without any planning permission, we know that the value is subjective. If they purchased the land recently, then the value may not have changed at all.

Another thing you can do at this stage is speak to the owner to see if they might be interested in jointly developing the site. If they are, then there may exist the potential to do the deal together. However, there are things to consider before you jump straight into a joint venture with a landowner, or anyone for that matter. Joint ventures need to be carefully considered and due diligence done with whomever you look to joint venture with, particularly if you did not know them beforehand.

The Title Plan shows you the size of the plot, something that is not always easy to judge from the road or even onsite. This helps assess what the potential of the site might be. This is where you can consult your planning consultant and/or architect, do your due diligence, and get a better understanding of the value of the site.

Here is an example of the letter that we send to landowners:

Ref: *Land on [Location] Title Number: [No.]*

Dear [Name],

I am writing to you in regards to the land on [Location], Title Number: [No.] of which, according to the land registry database, you are the owner.

White Box Property Solutions Ltd are a local property company owned by my business partner Andi Cooke and me. We have previously developed properties in and around Northamptonshire. We are looking for our next property development project and came across this land that you own.

Would you be interested in discussing a possible purchase or joint venture to develop this land to help meet the ever-increasing demand for properties? As a local to [Town name], I understand the importance of keeping our town a desirable place to live.

If you are interested, I would be delighted to arrange a meeting with you to not only share with you what we have done in the past but also to see if there would be any synergy in working together.

Please feel free to check out our website, www.whiteboxps.com. I look forward to hearing from you soon.

Yours sincerely,

Lloyd Girardi

Director

I want to set you a challenge and I hope you take it on. You have the letter and you now know how to find land opportunities via Google Maps. If you know of a site near you, send a letter. What's the worst that can happen? In fact, I challenge you to send five letters. That's all. Let me know how you get on at info@whiteboxps.com.

If you don't fancy all of that searching, and going onto the land registry database, looking for land and titles and waiting to receive the Title Plan, there is a terrific website called Land Insight, www.landinsight.io, designed to help you easily streamline your search for off-market deals. LandInsight shows you the land title plan. It can measure the area in an instant. It will give you the comparable sold properties in the street, and sometimes it will tell you what price per square foot those comparable properties sold for. It also tells you if the site is in a flood zone and gives you an idea of how tall the surrounding buildings are.

Not only can this site help you to find a plot of land but it can help you in your site appraisals too. Once you have found a plot of land, you can categorise it into various sections: a saved site, an opportunity site, a letter-sent section, and then, if you close on the deal, a final section, deal completed. Even better, you can customise the titles of these sections to better suit your needs and even add additional sections, if needed.

LandInsight is a fantastic new tool which can be used in a way similar to Google Maps, but it gives you so much more in the way of finding and analysing a deal quickly. It is a paid service, but worth the fee if you want to find development opportunities off market. There is a professional version as well which allows you to see recent planning applications, sold prices locally for comparison, ownership details, including contact details of the owners, property information, and a very handy work flow tool which allows you to save and track the status of a development site.

Councils

Your local council are your friends. Most will have a bank of brownfield (past use) sites they have already identified which they want to see redeveloped. Some may be in their development plan. And sometimes you can search for these on the council's website. This is a great source to finding opportunities that the council have highlighted. Some sites will have since been developed whilst others may not be up for sale or tender yet.

All councils have both a planning department and a planning portal on their website where all planning applications, past and present, are documented. Using the portal, you can find which plots have had planning applied for in the past. This is a good idea to do before purchasing the land registry documents previously mentioned. Some may have had planning which has lapsed; some may have had planning applications refused. It's a good due diligence process to perform.

You can search applications on the portal by week, an under-the-radar technique to capture developments that might be put onto the market once a planning decision has been granted, enabling you to perhaps get ahead of the game and negotiate a deal before a plot hits the market. This is definitely a numbers game, as not all planning applications are on sites intended for the market, but the possibility is such that it still makes it an off-market deal-finding tactic worth pursuing.

Searching the planning portal for refused planning applications, those less than a year old, can also be a good move, because if it's within a year, you can appeal and potentially overturn the refused planning decision. With planning applications, you get a 'free go' to re-submit the application with amendments designed to help it get through planning.

A refused planning application lists the reasons it was refused. Think of it as a checklist for your planning consultant or architect to overturn. The applicant is the one who has to submit the free go, but you may be able to assist them using your planning consultant's knowledge to get the planning they require. Again, not a tactic that is going to get loads and loads of deals, but one that might still pick up a few deals. If you're not doing it, you will never get deals.

Auctions

As noted in the beginning of the book, Andi and I found our very first site in St James, Northampton, via a local auction. Auctions are a fantastic way to find property development deals. What is great about auctions is that a lot of the legal work and some of the required local searches have already been done. You can download the legal pack from the auctioneer's website, or request a copy, and give it to your solicitor to read through to see if there is anything you need to be wary of. Any members of your power team, as appropriate, can also go through the legal pack and give you their expert opinion on the development site prior to the auction.

You want to do as much due diligence prior to the auction as possible, as you learned already from our story in chapter 1. Once the hammer goes down, the highest bidder is legally required to complete on the purchase within 28 days. So, you need to be confident in what you are bidding for. Auctions are good, as you can potentially pick up a good deal if you've done your homework.

Another way to use auctions to your advantage is by searching for all the unsold lots following an auction. The people looking to sell at auction have already demonstrated they want a quick sale. They anticipated selling within 28 days of the auction, so they are motivated.

If a site doesn't sell at auction, the seller is likely disappointed, perhaps even more anxious to sell. By searching for unsold lots, you may be able to negotiate a deal on the property site. The seller might even be willing to take a lower offer than the reserve price. Note that purchasing after auction still adheres to auction conditions, and you are required to complete your purchase within 28 days.

At auctions, the reserve price is generally set 10% higher than the guide price, so you can estimate the reserve price before the auction is held.

Deal sourcers

If lack of time or patience inhibits you from searching for land opportunities, you can use companies or individuals who specialise in finding land opportunities. Typically, you pay around 2% of the asking price as a finder's fee, but that's a rule of thumb. Fees can vary for different reasons. Depending on the quality of the deal, the price may be higher or lower.

A good sourced deal is one that is off-market and exclusive to you. Even if all the due diligence work is presented as having been done, it is imperative that you do your due diligence too. Deal sourcers are looking to sell plots, and so they may inflate some of their figures to make it look more attractive to potential buyers. Never purchase a site that you haven't done your own due diligence on first. I'm not saying that all deal sourcers inflate prices, but I can tell you that as a former salesman, I know this to be a sales tactic. I'm here to help and protect you.

Before you do any deal with a sourcer that sells deals, please check that they have the following:

- Data protection

- Registration with HMRC for anti-money laundering

- Registration with the property ombudsman

- Fit-for-purpose deal-brokering public indemnity insurance

Power team members

Your power team can function as more than just a power team for your developments once they're underway. They can also serve as your ears and ears on the ground, looking for potential development opportunities on your behalf. Your builder may learn about land opportunities from other jobs they've done, your solicitor may deal with repossessions, your accountant may deal with liquidations, your commercial financial broker may know people ranging from those struggling to fund their deals to the crème de la crème, and your architect may be doing the drawings for a landowner that could turn out to be your next development.

It is important to keep your power team close. If you have a good relationship with your architect, and other architects in your area, you may be able to pick up some off-market deals from them. They may know that their customer, the landowner, is looking to sell their development opportunity once they gain planning. This isn't uncommon. If you can speak to the landowner before they decide to go to the market, you have sourced an off-market deal.

There is a tenth way to find development land but it's not in the list above because to be fair, if you find yourself doing this, the reason is never going to be to look for land as it is way too much fun. The tenth way is to fly around as a passenger in a helicopter or a small plane.

With these other nine ways, however, you will be able to find a development opportunity. You are the only person who can stop you finding land. The people who are willing to put in the necessary effort to find land are the ones who end up with deals. If you think you can just log on to the internet, search for half an hour, and find a viable site, you will be disappointed. Finding land takes time, but the time you invest will pay you substantial dividends at the end of a development.

Once you get the hang of finding deals, appraising them, and offering what you can pay for the sites, you will have built a pipeline for opportunities. Remember, only offer on a site what you can justify paying for it, and not what the vendor wants. It has to work for you, and a lot of the good deals are made at the purchase stage of a development.

It's a numbers game

Finding deals is a numbers game, and so here is a structure to follow to best exploit that. Bearing in mind that there were 977 development opportunities within 40 miles of Northampton on one search, you must concentrate on your goldmine area. A more refined and concentrated search generated 86 potential development opportunities in Northampton alone.

This is just from a website search. This doesn't include opportunities found by speaking to agents, councils, architects, deal sourcers, auctions, land registry letters, etc. You may have a hundred potential opportunities. Use my 30/10 principle each month to offer on sites.

The 30/10 principle

The 30/10 principle is simply taking the hundred-odd sites that you have sourced and categorising them, using the traffic light system modelled after your initial desktop appraisal:

- Green sites: You would willingly offer up to 10% below asking

- Amber sites: You would only offer between 11% and 30% below asking price

- Red sites: The deal only makes sense to offer less than 70% of the asking price

Place an offer on those sites you have designated green and amber. Once an offer gets accepted, the money doesn't come straight out of your account, so don't be afraid to offer on a desktop appraisal. You can use the 'subject to full site appraisal within two weeks of offer being accepted' condition when you place an offer based on a desktop appraisal. It puts your interest in the deal and gives you time to do your full site appraisal.

You want to be appraising 30 deals a month and offering on a minimum of 10. If you can do that every month, that's 360 appraised deals and 120 offers a year. Do you think you will get an offer accepted out of that? This is your pipeline.

What if only five per cent of your offers are accepted? That's six accepted offers in a year. What if you went on to develop two of those deals yourself and sold the other four acting as a deal sourcer for a finder's fee of 2% of the asking price? An average small development site, depending on your location, may be around £600,000 asking price each. Four of them would total £2,400,000. If you sold all four for 2%, that's £48,000 gross profit – and that's just on 5% of your offers being accepted. Imagine if 10% were accepted. Imagine 20%. Sourcing deals can be rewarding in itself.

Keep a log of the offers you make and expect them to be declined. Yes, declined. Don't expect them to be accepted. If they are, that's great. Remember, you are offering on what you can pay, and that may be less than the asking price, so the chances of the offer being accepted may be slim unless the seller is motivated and the property has been on the market for a while. What we are doing with the 30/10 principle is creating a pipeline. This pipeline will feed your deals.

Please let me know if you take on the 30/10 principle and how you get on. Tweet me at @whiteboxps using the hashtag #thirtytenprinciple. Or join our Facebook community on the group Property Developers Secrets. If you get any decent deals that you are looking to sell, let me know there as well. If we don't buy them from you, we might know someone else who would.

Making an offer

Whether you make the offer to an estate agent, landowner, or friend, the way you should pose your offer should always be the same.

Your traditional buy-to-let investor may make an offer over the phone or by emailing it on a single line. That's not what we do. Some people may see what we do as tipping our hand, or leaving all of our cards face up on the table, but we feel this makes our offer stronger. Landowners may sometimes overprice their land because they don't actually know how much it is worth. (They need to read this book.)

The way we offer is the way we advise you to make offers. Show the estate agent/ landowner/ friend why you can only pay what you have offered for the site. Show them that you have calculated the end value based on what the area is currently demanding. Show them that you have factored in your build costs and contingencies. Show them that you have factored in profit for yourself.

Yes, show them the profit you intend to make. If we're working on 25% profit, then we show them that. At the end of the day, you need to make money on a project in order to make it worth buying.

Some of you may read this and think that showing our

calculations is crazy, even self-defeating, but in fact it isn't – it can give you a distinct advantage. We have received feedback equally from estate agents and landowners who were impressed by our willingness to do this. Who doesn't want to do business with someone who's open and honest, serious and thoughtful, and who isn't looking to waste their time? On occasion, we have won deals precisely because of our honesty and openness.

On one particular deal, we were one of 16 offers on the site. What set us apart from the other 15 buyers was that we were the only one to create and send an offer pack illustrating our value breakdown, our development goal, and the profit we needed to make in order to justify doing the deal to the agents – not a single line in an email, or a phone call. A pack. We create ours in PowerPoint and save it as a PDF.

After we submitted our offer pack, the agent whittled the 16 offers down to the four he felt were serious. Ours was one of them.

Do you think had we just sent a one-line email with 'Our offer is £750,000', we would have made the top four and be considered serious buyers? Possible, yes. Likely, no. What credibility would that give us? We were making an offer for a serious project, a development site.

The agent needs to convince the landowner that you are legitimate, and that you are capable of completing on the purchase. That means you need to first convince the agent of this. Creating an offer pack gives you professional credibility, something not everyone does (apart from those who have read this book or we have trained, that is.)

You should include the following in every offer pack:

- Front cover

- 'About you' information

- Outline of the site

- Your offer (include your calculation breakdowns)

- Comparable properties' recent sale/closing (not asking) prices

- Track record of any previous deals (if you haven't any, reference those of your builders or other power team members)

- Solicitor's details

Creating and submitting an offer pack has the additional benefit of building rapport with agents. Some comments we've received from estate agents after submitting an offer pack include, 'I have never seen an offer presented so professionally before' and 'Wow, this offer pack actually explains the reasons justifying your offering price!' Some agents have even taken a closer look and said, 'Hmm, maybe the land really is only worth what you've offered'.

Offer packs work. Ultimately, the owner accepted our offer on the site with the original 16 offers. That development is scheduled to make us between £700,000 and £900,000. Not bad for the time it took to put together our offer pack.

The Round–Round–Random offer method

When making offers it is important to remember that it is a negotiation. When you sell something, you tend to price it higher than the amount you actually want to give you room to negotiate. When you buy something, you give yourself that same room and offer less than what you expect to have to pay. This doesn't change, even when buying land.

A technique we use when calculating and making offers is

what's called the Round–Round–Random method. We have already identified how much we can pay for a particular plot of land, the price that works for us. It's the price we can afford to pay but might be considerably lower than the asking price. So, to support the offer we make, we apply the three-step Round–Round–Random method.

How it works

Let's say we can afford to pay £600,000 for a plot of land. Our initial offer is a round number below that, perhaps £550,000. That's offer number one. Now, let's assume that offer has been declined.

Our next offer is higher – another round number, say, £570,000. If this is accepted, then that's fantastic. If not, our final offer is a random number. Bearing in mind we know we can pay around £600,000, we offer something like £587,623.

What does this kind of precision say to the landowner? That, psychologically, we have put everything we can into the deal to make it work. If we said another nice round number like £600,000, then the landowner or agent will assume we can keep going up, nearer the asking price.

If you keep offering nice round numbers, you encourage the agent or landowner to continue to ask for price increases. Remember one of the property purchase golden rules: Buy with your head, not with your heart.

Property developments more rewarding than single lets

Are you a property investor already? Have you stuck to single buy-to-lets or houses of multiple occupancy (HMOs)?

If not an investor yet, you could start like we did, straight into developments. Anyone reading this book already possesses more knowledge about the process and how to safeguard against pitfalls than we did when we started.

Here's something for you to think about – and I mean to seriously think about, for your own benefit – if you do or are considering buy-to-lets. Let's look at the time and energy typically required for single buy-to-lets, HMOs, and new-build developments, so you can see the potential that lies in new-build developments. The following chart illustrates the differences between these, assuming each with a purchase price of £200,000, based on actual prices at the time the chart was created.

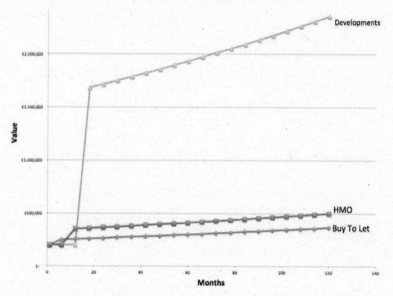

On the x or horizontal axis, along the bottom, is plotted the average number of months necessary to get each project completed.

Running up the side, along the y or vertical axis, is the value, from the initial purchase on day one to the completion of all improvements.

The single buy-to-let property is a 3-bed semi-detached property, the HMO is a 4-bed terraced house to be converted into a 6-bed HMO, and the new-build development site is vacant land, mimicking a development we completed of eleven 2-bed houses.

As you can see, the single buy-to-let takes around three months to renovate and another three months to refinance. After spending some money, maybe £20–30,000, to convert the property, we assume it might be worth about £250,000 once completed.

The HMO takes about six months to convert, a bit more invested in improvements (say, £50–60,000), and potentially three months to refinance, ending up with a commercial value of around £350,000.

The new-build site takes an estimated 12 months to build and six months to refinance. The difference here, although the development takes longer, is that it has a value of £1,684,000, based on eleven 2-bed houses. That's 86% higher than the single buy-to-let, and 80% higher than the HMO, for an investment of an additional 12 months to finish versus the single buy-to-let, and nine months more than the HMO.

Victoria Street, Irthlingborough

Our second deal, following the St James project, was a site on Victoria Street, in Irthlingborough. It went extraordinarily well. Whilst developing the St James site, which we'd begun in September 2014, we had taken some potential investors there to show them what we were doing. (You will find that once you get underway, people will be watching what you do, possibly in hopes of investing in your next deal.)

One investor we showed the St James site to, who now invests with us, had a friend who owned an estate agency and tipped us off to a plot of land in the town I lived in at the time that was for sale. It turned out to have been on the market for a while and had been listed on Rightmove, but because we had been focused the past three or four months on completing our first development deal, we were not paying attention to any other properties being sold. The owner had recently taken the plot off the market.

Andi went to have a look at it. It looked good. It was local, we knew the area very well, and the price seemed reasonable. We arranged through the agent to meet the owner in a pub opposite the St James development, and showed him around our current project, figuring it would demonstrate that we were serious.

We agreed to purchase the site in December 2014 for £180,000, with a delayed completion of June 2015 to give us sufficient time to finish the St James development and ideally convince our St James investors to invest in this next site.

The following February, the owner advised us that there was another offer on the table. Despite having agreed to sell it to us, we did not have any contractual agreement, so it wasn't unethical for him to entertain another offer. The offer was about £30,000 more that we'd agreed to pay. He would sell it to us, he said, if we could up our price to £200,000 and complete in four weeks instead of four months.

I love a challenge. Admittedly, I was still trying to prove myself as much to Andi, to convince him of the wisdom of having asked me to partner in property investing as I was myself. He had owned a business since 2007 whilst I was new to entrepreneurship. Andi and I have always been competitive. We even installed a table-tennis table in our office. Loser makes the tea, and so on. Whenever we have a stalemate, off to the table tennis table we go. I like this set-up, as Andi invariably ends up having to make the tea.

So, because it was early on, I was still discovering my capabilities and where my talents lay. I love the analytical side and love interacting with people. So I assumed responsibility for raising the £200,000 required, using our model of owning the land outright using private investor finance and then covering all of the development costs through development finance lenders.

I said to Andi, 'If I don't find the £200,000 within two weeks, I'll wash your car'.

'In a tutu', he added.

I thought about it for a moment and agreed. Looking back, I don't know why but I suppose a slight bit of arrogance came out and I thought, I can do this. I had faith in myself. It was February 14th, 2015, and my in-laws were having a Valentine's Day party at their house. Little did I realise how fortuitous that would turn out to be.

That evening, I met one of my in-laws' friends, an ex-banker who had retired early and played golf pretty much every day. (Sounded awesome.) I was telling him about the St James deal and he was very interested. I found myself wondering whether he might be interested in investing, but hesitated. I thought to myself, I can't ask him – I don't know him!

I was still a bit uncomfortable asking people to invest their money in me, something that is not uncommon and is frequently cited to us as a reason why people hesitate doing developments. We were no different. We were new to it all back then.

I thought about how I could ask him for money without actually asking him and decided the best way would be to tell him how we structured our previous development. After all, we were copying what we had done the last time. I mentioned how we'd raised money through Funding Circle. He had heard of them, as he had a friend who invested with them, and asked how it worked.

BOOM! This is my time, I thought. This is how I can ask for money without asking for money. I can ask whether his friend might be interested in investing. That way I'm not asking him directly to invest, yet giving him an opening. Brilliant.

I found out that his friend made about a 6% return on his Funding Circle investments, and casually dropped that we had a development project due to start in June which would pay 10% interest. The conversation focused only on his friend and how the deal would work to pay his friend back.

The following morning, I phoned the retired banker to follow up and ask if he would pass on my details or give me his friend's contact information.

'Forget my friend', he said. 'I would be interested in investing.'

Ta ta, tutu, I thought, grinning.

I am very much a visual person, so, for me, the best way to explain something is to illustrate it on paper. I sat down and created an investor pack to explain the deal. We estimated the gross development value figures very conservatively, listed the rental income and comparable property values in the area, and included the site plan and a layout. I had 3D images created by a guy in Slovakia from a website called Fiverr.com. (Fiverr is great for getting anything done for US$5.00, or roughly £3.62, currently.)

As a result of the investor pack, the ex-banker offered to invest

£100,000 into our deal, our biggest single investment thus far. I was delighted. We were halfway there. But I still had another £100,000 to go.

I approached a few other people whom I knew would potentially be interested and secured a further £50,000. At that point, I was six days away from my deadline, and the inevitable tutu-clad car wash was looming.

I followed up with a few more people who had showed some initial interest and eventually nailed down another £25,000. I had £25,000 to go, and just two days to get it. Did I make it?

No.

Did I end up washing Andi's car in a tutu?

No.

But I did end up washing it in a Gerry Hallowell Union Jack Spice Girls outfit, because we didn't have a tutu. (Yes, if you are a visual person, like me, I apologise for the image you've got in your head right now.) I'd raised £175,000 in just two weeks, more than 85% of what we needed, but I was still £25,000 short. And Andi was not about to let me have an extension.

As it turned out, I found the remaining £25,000 about three days after I'd washed the car, still within our required four-week deadline.

Purchase Price (including planning for 11 houses)	£200,000
Development Costs	£750,000
Total Spend	£1,045,000
Gross Development Value	£1,684,000
Mortgage (63% LTV)	£1,061,346
Profit	£639,000
Monthly gross rental income	£8,800
Monthly net income after costs	£4,600

We completed the Victoria Street site in June 2016, fifteen months after we'd completed the site purchase. To our astonishment and delight, our project was later nominated as a finalist for 'Deal of the Year' at the Property Investors Awards 2016, an incredible achievement. We were runners-up in the end but felt enormously honoured to have been nominated. And that was after our St James development had won 'Deal of The Year' 2014, by the Progressive Property Community of which we were part of then.

The way we went about this development site was no different to our first development site. This was for eleven houses, so the numbers were a bit bigger than the first site but the method was the same.

We raised 100% of the land purchase price through private investments on loan agreements and the remaining build costs and other fees using development finance and Funding Circle.

Our exit was exactly the same, although this time, rather than a 75% loan-to-value mortgage, we were able to take a 63% loan-to value mortgage, as that was enough money to pay back all of our investors and the outstanding development finance.

The most interesting thing about a postage stamp is the persistence with which it sticks to its job. –Napoleon Hill

Secret Tip #10: If you stick to the 30/10 principle, development deals will come. One of every two deals falls out of bed when it comes to commercial developments, so don't give up. Build your pipeline and proactively chase your offers up every three months.

Chapter 9 Finance a Deal Using None of Your Own Money

Before going into the details of how you can become a property developer using none of your own money, I need to share some important information.

Borrowing money or receiving investments always presents a risk to both you and the individual, business, or fund making the loan. Any investment should always be given careful consideration by both parties. Before entering any joint venture agreement, look at all the possible eventualities. How much can you afford to lose if it all goes wrong?

When we first started. I didn't have any savings to draw on to pay back our investors, and I didn't have any assets that I could use to support a personal guarantee. Neither did Andi. The only thing we did have was the equity in our own homes. I had about £40,000 equity at the time and Andi had about £100,000.

We borrowed over £750,000 for our first development. Funding Circle, the development finance lender, took a first charge on the site as security, and our private lenders were given no security. They were friends and family to start with, so they didn't demand any security, a good thing as we were not yet in a position to offer any. But they believed in us, they could see that the development site had enough profit in it that were we forced to sell the site at the end rather than keep it, they would still get their money back.

Nowadays, when we receive investment from private investors, we ask what security they would like. The only thing we can't offer, unless they front the entire purchase and development finance, is a first charge. A development finance lender will always take a first charge over a development.

Secured and unsecured loans

Secured borrowing is backed by some form of legal security. This includes first, second, and sequential charges, and a personal guarantee.

A first charge, or first legal charge, is a legal charge over the development that is registered with a solicitor and land registry. A lender possessing a first charge has the primary legal right to funds available from the sale of the development, not to exceed the amount owed. (This may, depending on the situation, include additional funds from any arrears, costs, and legal charges, plus other fees that have accrued, such as in the event of a repossession.)

A second charge is simply a charge that ranks below the first charge lender. The second charge comes into play when the first charge lender has received all of their investment funds back, in the event of repossession or sale. If the first charge lender takes more than their initial investment amount as reimbursement for additional costs, this may further limit the amount available against which the second charge lender can claim.

A personal guarantee (PG) is just that – the individual(s) borrowing the money have offered a personal guarantee to repay what they've borrowed, which is a legally enforceable personal pledge to repay that debt. The individual(s) may have to refinance or liquidate any assets they have in order to pay back the outstanding debt. Typically, in property investment, the PG is unsecured, which means the guarantee is signed but no charges are placed over other assets you own, unlike business loans where banks often take a charge on an asset to back up the PG.

When borrowing money, you should always be careful to comply with all rules and regulations. That said, money is lent and borrowed all the time, so it is not something to be nervous about. The rules and regulations are there to protect all parties, lenders and borrowers.

Profit-sharing

One thing you must decide is whether you intend to borrow money on a loan agreement or in exchange for a share in the profits. If the latter, you need to familiarise yourself with a particular, relevant directive of the Financial Conduct Authority (FCA), the Policy Statement 13/3, or PS13/3,[8] which was introduced in January 2014. The directive protects retail customers from making investments which have not been approved or regulated by the FCA that can fall beyond their level of understanding.

Borrowing money using a loan agreement is something that is not regulated by the FCA. You can talk to any Tom, Dick, or Harry about a loan, as the FCA see it as a straightforward monetary transaction between two parties who should understand what a loan is: I lend you £x and in exchange you give me x + y (interest back) in z months'/years' time. Simple.

When a share in profits or equity is offered instead, the PS13/3 directive applies. Such an arrangement is regulated by the FCA as it is deemed to be a more complicated transaction, and the FCA don't want retail customers, i.e., ordinary investors, to get caught out.

You cannot mention any equity share or profit splits unless you can first clarify that the individual lending you the money is either a high-net-worth individual (HNWI) or sophisticated investor. What constitutes such a classification?

A potential investor needs to meet at least one of these criteria:

8 See https://www.fca.org.uk/publication/policy/ps13-03. pdf.

- Possess an annual income of at least £100,000

- Possess net assets of at least £250,000 (excluding the equity in one's own home)

- Be classified as a professional investor, considered to possess extensive investment experience and knowledge of complex instruments, capable of understanding and evaluating the associated risks and potential rewards of unusual, complex, and/ or illiquid investments (e.g., a money trader or stockbroker)

- Be a director of a business with an annual turnover of £1 million-plus

- Operate as an 'angel investor' (affluent individuals who inject capital into business start-ups) in exchange for ownership equity or convertible debt

There are two exemptions to requiring this of your investors when offering profit share: when the investors are either family members or longstanding friends.

Further information on investment compliance can be obtained from a good friend of ours, Kevin Wright, of Positive Property Finance.[9]

How to acquire the required equity

Once you have determined the most suitable way(s) for you to borrow money, there are various options to consider for both purchase and development finance lending. Generally, you are required to invest some equity into the deal before you can get development finance from lenders. This is not to be confused

---

9   Contact Kevin Wright at kevinwright@thinkpositively. co.uk, or telephone him at 01206 586 586.

with the equity that exists at the end of a development, using the build-to-rent model.

Let's say the initial equity required is 20% of the total cost of the development. The lenders will give you 80% of the development costs (the debt part) assuming they are happy with the development plans and the people involved. There are many ways you can inject the necessary equity into the deal, even when you have no money.

Bridging loans

Despite the negative reputation this type of finance has, it is actually a very powerful tool to have in your kit bag. Bridging is essentially short-term finance taken for a number of months, before either selling or refinancing to repay it. Associated rates are higher than those of mortgages, so you need to have a clear plan in place to repay the loan in the shortest time possible.

Unlike how mortgages get underwritten, bridging loans work in the opposite way in many respects. Bridging is asset-based, rather than income-based lending, i.e., it is more about the property than the person. Bridging lenders will lend on pretty much any condition of property, unlike mortgage lenders. Bridging lenders also tend to be fast, enabling you to offer sellers of development sites a faster completion, and that is often what secures the deal.

Typical loan-to-value loans comprise 70–75% of the purchase price; however, some bridging lenders are happy to lend against current value/asking price rather than purchase price, something that can be handy when you have negotiated a discounted purchase.

One of our students recently purchased a site for £235,000 that was valued at £430,000. He got a 65% loan-to-value on the higher figure, the actual value of the land, rather than the purchase price, which meant his loan amount came to £268,000, less some fees, which exceeded what he had agreed to pay for it. That meant our student was able to purchase 100% of the land costs with the bridging loan that he will pay off through private investor finance.

Crowdfunding

We talked about this earlier, in chapter 3, concerning how we funded the St James development and our Victoria Street project. Crowdfunding is a newer type of funding that has gained in popularity post credit crunch. Its use is wider than just property investment, and SMEs (small and medium-sized enterprises) can now use it as an alternative to business loans from the typical high street banks.

In property terms, it is still fairly early days yet, but crowdfunding offers would-be developers an opportunity to get their development funded, as well as giving small-time investors an opportunity to achieve a potentially favourable return on a modest capital investment. With some crowdfunding platforms, the maximum loan amount is not as high as those offered by development finance lenders.

An advantage of crowdfunding finance is it is generally pre-funded, rather than retrospectively funded as is the case with almost all development finance lenders.

Angel Finance

This again transcends property and is available in the wider business world. It tends to comprise private individuals rather than companies, and those with a higher tolerance to risk who are willing to bankroll a company or investment. Sometimes the return offered to angel investors is a stake in the company if it is a longer collaboration, or a share of the profits if it is more on a project-by-project basis. Angels tend to be high-net-worth individuals who often have multiple people pitching for their time and money, a bit like the reality show Dragon's Den, so you need to be on the ball to interest them in investing with you.

Private Investors

These are similar to angel investors, but they operate on a smaller scale and possess more modest capital means. Sometime they prefer to invest in exchange for a share of the profits; other times it will be on a fixed-interest loan basis.

For profit sharing, remember that this falls within the remit of FCA directive PS13/3 mentioned earlier, which governs not only who can invest but who can be marketed to, with respect to FCA unregulated investments. You must do the appropriate due diligence on investors in this case.

If you borrow money on a loan agreement basis, which is unregulated, the FCA PS13/3 directive does not apply.

Refinance existing assets

If you already own property, be it your main residence or investment properties, you might be able to increase your borrowing on them in order to increase your available cash pile for property investing.

Borrowing additional funds against your main residence can be accomplished by a) getting a further advance from your current lender, which would extend over the life of the original loan, b) re-mortgaging in full with a new lender, or c) taking out an addition loan secured on your property as a second charge whilst not disturbing the first-positioned loan lender.

You will be subject to underwriting restrictions on the amount you can borrow, and what extra you can borrow may be subject to what level of income you can prove you earn.

You may also be able to refinance investment properties you own, again with the same a/b/c options as above. The rental income such properties generate will determine the extent of the borrowing you can secure.

Another short-term option would be to use bridging finance against your current assets, but you must be in a position to repay the loan within a matter of months.

Equity release

Be careful about mentioning the term 'equity release' to a mortgage broker. In their parlance it refers to reverse-mortgaging, finance taken out by those over age fifty, who are property asset rich and cash poor and want to supplement their retirement income in their later years by conveying ownership of their asset(s) to the lender after their death.

In property circles, it means something different – pulling equity out of properties you own to add to your cash pot for investing. In other words, it is what has already been covered in the preceding section on refinancing existing assets.

Vendor Finance

Sometimes, one of the best ways to avoid having to secure money to purchase a plot of land is to enter into a joint venture directly with the landowner. By using the Land Registry search, you can find direct-to-vendor deals and speak to the landowners directly.

It might be that a landowner has been thinking of developing on their land but never knew how, or perhaps didn't have the confidence. You may spark their interest with a letter. If you arrange a meeting with them and discuss the potential to purchase the plot, they might even suggest a joint venture. Or you might suggest it.

If this is the case and the landowner has no encumbrance (mortgage) on the land, then one possibility is to have the landowner contribute the land as their portion of the deal while you obtain the development finance. One advantage in this case is that you won't have to spend time and effort securing any private investment money.

The easiest way to do this is to bring the landowner into the SPV (special purpose vehicle, as covered in chapter 4) as a shareholder. The landowner must permit the development finance lender to take a first charge over the plot. What the landowner stands to get out of the deal is the agreed price for the land to be paid on completion of the development, plus their share in the business.

Clarifying the FCA PS13/3 directive should be relatively straightforward, as you would be purchasing an asset (the land) from them which could be valued at more than £250,000.

Once you have the equity required to do the development, securing the development finance portion is fairly straightforward. Again, lenders are in business to lend money. Lenders all have different criteria, so depending on your deal, its location, your personal situation, history, and other aspects, you more than likely will have several lender options available to you. Choosing a lender most often boils down to cost and timescale considerations.

Development Finance

Development finance is how most developments are funded. These lenders specialise in development and commercial projects, and most of the time it is the deal that the lender is concerned with, rather than the individual or company applying for the funds.

These lenders will want to know about you, and what you have done in the past, but inevitably it's the deal itself that needs to stack up.

The lenders will do their own due diligence on your development deal to ensure they get their money back. Some lenders only deal with development funding needs above £1 million, whereas others lend starting at £250,000.

Most lenders require past development experience; however, a few are happy to lend to first-time developers. In this case, they are interested not just in the deal but who is doing the deal. Your power team is key in this situation. And because the risk they're assuming is greater, you will be required to pay more interest for the privilege, but they are available.

When you lack experience, there are other ways to encourage development lenders to lend. Every scenario has a solution. Find someone who has the experience you currently lack. Look to possible joint ventures (keeping in mind the FCA directives) and consider who you are joint venturing with. Although I didn't have development experience, Andi did.

On your first development, don't be afraid to give more away to get you started. Everyone started somewhere, so why should you be any different?

Development finance tranches

Once you have a lender on board and have completed the underwriting stage, you will go through a process before getting your first tranche or drawdown. Development finance is always broken down into tranches. The amount of the tranches differs depending on your lender, but generally you decide how frequently you require the tranches. The more tranches you elect to have, the more fees you will pay for a monitoring surveyor to assess the process of the development, something that is required by the lender. The project monitoring surveyor (PMS) is an independent surveyor who is appointed by the lender to ensure the development is progressing in conjunction with the lending. The PMS is usually the same as the initial PMS, when the lender did their initial due diligence on the development.

Development finance is paid in arrears so you may require some additional funds to start your development.

Home Building Fund

The Home Building Fund is a flexible source of funding administered by the Homes and Communities Agency (HCA) on behalf of government. The fund provides development finance as a loan facility to meet the development costs of building homes for sale or rent. Its total budget is currently £3 billion.

There are criteria to meet, but the Home Building Fund is there to help developments that are harder to fund through traditional development finance. The Home Building Fund isn't entirely location-driven, like some lenders, although there are certain areas where they won't lend in, like within the M25 and greater Manchester. This is another option for finance but, again, this still requires an equity investment from the developer. We have a couple of sites at the moment where we have agreement in principle for funding, a site for 12 houses and one to convert a former office building into 18 high-end apartments.

It's not how much money you make, but how much money you keep, how hard it works for you, and how many generations you keep it for. – Robert Kiyosaki

Secret Tip #11: Don't let your self-doubt in finding investment money stop you finding development deals. Money follows deals.

Chapter 10 Starting Your Property Development Build

You've done it! Your offer has been accepted, you've completed on the purchase of the site, your development finance is in place and ready to be drawn down, and you know your budget for construction. You have had the necessary searches done to make sure that the site is legally permitted to develop. And you have the required planning permission to develop.

In short, you have done every bit of due diligence needed before starting your development.

Now it's time to get it done.

Choosing a builder

Choosing your builder is an essential part of the development. The size of the development will determine what size construction company you require. You need to understand what type of contract you are looking for.

Do you want to go down the design-build procurement route? Or the traditional procurement route and ask contractors to submit tenders for the development?

The latter requires you, the client, to hire consultants to design the building followed by contractors to construct the works. There are merits to both approaches. The design-and-build route, which is easier on you, can be more expensive.

You could agree to a fixed-price contract with the contractor. One benefit to you is that you know the fixed cost of your project, so any overspend will not be borne by you. The downside is that a contractor will inevitably factor in some kind of contingency within that fixed price to cover any overspend, so the price is higher. If it fits your budget, it's worth considering.

If you choose to select individual consultants and contractors for each stage of the build, a skilled project manager can help, saving you time and money.

Health and safety

A property development project needs very careful consideration of health and safety. A property development site is a construction site and there needs to be strict compliance to health and safety regulations.

As the developer, you must comply to the current Construction Design and Management regulations (CDM) 2015. It is your legal responsibility to ensure the health and safety of all who might be affected by the work, including members of the public.

Property developments fall under the category of a commercial client. Ensuring safety can be detailed and intense without the right team and processes in place.

Things you need to focus on include:

- How to access the site

- How to receive deliveries – what route will they take using a traffic management system?

- How do you plan to build? Left to right? Top to bottom? Clockwise/anticlockwise? Work out the best build route.

- Will you phase your development?

There are plenty of people out there who can guide you, such as a good project manager, and specific safety coordinators.

Once you have established the method of how you are going to construct, you must put together a construction phase plan to present to the Health and Safety Executive (HSE), the Government's independent regulators. It is good practice to state how the build will progress.

This is also guidance for the contractors to build in the safest manner. When you introduce contractors, main- or sub-contractors, you must ensure they have the relevant risk assessment and method statement and health and safety policies in place. Also, any subcontractor who works for you should have liability insurance relevant to the works they will be performing. You can find more information about this through the HSE government website, www.hse.gov.uk.

If your site is of the recognised size and working timescales, you should have your site registered with HSE under what is known as an F10 notification of construction works. HSE must be notified of any project defined as construction under the regulations where the construction work is likely to last longer than 30 working days and have more than 20 workers, working simultaneously at any point in the project, or exceed 500 person days.

The HSE are effectively the Government's police in managing health and safety onsite. Therefore, anyone, including trades onsite or members of the public, can report anything to HSE that they feel represents a danger to the public or the trades themselves. Please ensure that you always work within the parameters of the HSE guidance.

There are fundamental roles, as stated by the HSE, for the management of safety onsite:

Principle Designer – A designer appointed by the client to control the pre-construction phase on projects with more than one contractor. The principal designer's main duty is to plan, manage, monitor, and coordinate health and safety during this phase when most design work is carried out.

Principle Contractor – A contractor appointed by the client to manage the construction phase on projects employing more than one contractor. The principal contractor's main duty is to plan, manage, monitor, and coordinate health and safety during this phase when all construction work takes place.

Contractor – An individual or business in charge of carrying out construction work (e.g., building, altering, maintaining, or demolishing). Anyone who manages this work or directly employs or engages construction workers is a contractor. Their main duty is to plan, manage, and monitor the work under their control in a way that ensures the health and safety of anyone it might affect (including members of the public). Contractors work under the control of the principal contractor on projects with more than one contractor.

Worker – An individual who physically carries out the work involved in building, altering, maintaining, or demolishing buildings or structures. Workers include plumbers, electricians, scaffolders, painters, decorators, steel erectors, and labourers, as well as supervisors like foremen and chargehands. Their duties include cooperating with their employer and other dutyholders, and reporting anything they see that might endanger the health and safety of themselves or others. Workers must be consulted on matters affecting their health, safety, and welfare.

Again, this information is available on the HSE website, www. hse.gov.uk. Everyone has a responsibility to look after themselves and others under the health and safety regulations.

In the twelve years that our project manager Nick has worked in construction management, he has never yet had any issues or direct involvement with HSE, having worked under a strict health and safety regime with one of the UK's biggest builders, something he continues to uphold now, for our developments. Nick looks after the health and safety side of our developments to the best of standards, and Andi oversees Nick's work to ensure everything is in order, because it is our responsibility, Andi's and mine, to ensure CDM is being adhered to.

Nick has seen several contractors and developers fall afoul of their actions when they were not working in accordance with the law. For example, he remembers one gentleman operating a disc cutter, known as a Stihl saw, with no face mask, eye or ear protection, or dust suppression. A savvy local resident called the HSE and reported him, after which an inspector came and shut down all of the works, pending an enquiry.

Once you get an inspector on your site, if something is wrong, you can be sure they will find it. Violations result in the issuance of enforcement notices and a fee charged for intervention to cover the time the inspector spends working on the issues related to your site. At the time of writing, this charge is £129 per hour.

As you can imagine, they are thorough. They identify the problems, put them right, and then charge for the office work too. This means that any time spent taking action will be charged, which could be days or weeks, depending on the issues.

Fatalities occasionally occur. Back in March 2017, it was reported that a worker on one site did not follow the HSE CDM plan of traffic management, was caught walking in the wrong place at the wrong time, and was knocked over and killed by a dumper truck. If the principle contractor had failed to induct him or have him signed up to the risk assessments, method statement, or traffic management plans for the site, then effectively they could have been liable for manslaughter under the corporate responsibilities.

If such an incident occurred on your development site, you are that contractor's client, which means you could be charged too if you are not in compliance. This happened in the instance above, and a court case is pending.

Do not let this be you. Onsite fatalities, according to the HSE, affect 1.62 of every 100,000 workers in the construction industry. The average fatality rate across all other industries is 0.46 per 100,000 workers, so it is 3.5 times more frequent in construction than in other industries. Almost half of the fatalities result from a fall from heights.

You can outsource the health and safety oversight of a property development site. There are several various safety bodies across the UK. One current qualification that allows people to give this advice is known as NEBOSH, the National Examination Board in Occupational Safety and Health.

If you outsource and instruct the design-build method, then generally the F10 will be their responsibility, but you can make sure they are doing the CDM regulations by hiring a NEBOSH-qualified representative to do a spot check. Consider doing this once a month to ensure everything is being handled responsibly.

Required onsite accommodations

Another legal requirement onsite is to make sure that you have various facilities at minimum available for your work force. Your main contractor may supply this as part of the package. Generally, you need to afford workers somewhere to rest, a means to warm up food (preferably a microwave), and a place to wash their hands in clean, warm water.

You need to have a facility where your workers can dry wet clothes, and you need toilets, separate men's and women's toilets if relevant.

If you have more than five workers onsite, you are required to furnish two onsite toilets.

All of the above can be a part of a welfare unit. Within this welfare unit, you will need first-aid equipment adequate for the amount of people on your site, along with someone onsite with basic first-aid training.

You also need to maintain a record of accidents, generally in an accident book or health and safety file, which is kept onsite. Some accidents will need to be recorded and reported to the HSE if they fall into the categories regulated under RIDDOR, the HSE's Reporting of Injuries, Diseases and Dangerous Occurrences Regulations 2013.

Managing your contractors onsite

When you get to the stage where work has begun onsite, contractors need direction. You want to ensure that you get the best out of your contractors and achieve the desired finish, so be sure to give them a detailed specification from the word go. All too often, extra costs are incurred or workers go off on a tangent because not enough specification was provided. This is something that Nick, our project manager, is fantastic at – the specifications that is, not going off on tangents.

Obviously, contractors know their own trade better than you do, but that doesn't mean you can overlook giving them precise direction on a certain specification or finish. This specification should be included in your tender pack, which will also get you a more accurate price.

Once you agree on the specification and price, you and your contractor should sign a mutual agreement (commonly known as a JCT contract). In simple terms, a JCT, which stands for Joint Contracts Tribunal, is a contract between you and a contractor, and is the most widely used form of contract in the construction industry. You should execute a JCT contract with every trade, unless you have a design-build main contractor, which only requires one JCT. Once your contracts are in place, you are ready to start your construction phase.

The contractor's programme of work

A programme of work is a rough guideline, with contingency for how long the works relevant to the contractor(s) are likely to take. To formulate the plan for the build, we create a flow chart which explains how long each particular phase should take.

Having a programme in place, and knowing roughly how long things will take, allows you to plan your finances more accurately. It illustrates how much work should be done and when, making it easier to keep track of your budget and manage your drawdown schedule from development finance or investors. The better the programme, the faster you reach completion, which enables you to save on interest on the money you draw.

Structural works warranties and approvals

Something you need to arrange early on is to have a building control body sign off on your site's structural works. There are various ways you can do this, including local authority building control through your council, or private contractors that are approved, such as NHBC and JHAI.

We use JHAI, because they work with our warranty provider, which saves us time and money by reducing delays on the build. Some of these contractors also offer structural warranty providers.

A structural warranty is a must for new-build developments. You will not be able to sign off your project, have tenants move in, or sell your units without one. You will need one for each property you build, so if you are building 10 units on one site, you need 10 structural warranties.

The warranty provider that we use is CRL (c-r-l.com). Each structural warranty provider performs various inspections throughout your build. The first is to ensure the drawings are acceptable as per the building regulations – that they conform to the most recent updates and safety criteria, such as smoke alarms and fire regulations. More recently, following the tragedy of Grenfell Tower, fire regulations have been stepped up and sprinkler systems are soon to be a requirement. These are all part of the national building regulations.

Onsite inspections

Clearing the site in preparation for development to begin means getting rid of, or consolidating, the top soil to dig, in most cases, the footings. These footings will be examined by your inspector as part of the building regulations requirements, and also for your structural warranty provider.

In the case of the NHBC and similar providers, they do the inspections in one hit. NHBC does both the building regulations and structural warranty inspections. Other contractors can do it on behalf of the provider.

Usually, if you dig a footing, you get the inspector out the following morning and pour later that day. The foundation block work and internal drains will be inspected as part of their remit to see how you have connected your drains to the ongoing runs.

The next inspection is known as the superstructure inspection. This is usually at a stage when the first-floor joists have been installed, so they can determine the consistency of the brickwork, internal block work, and cavities, the correct spacing of brick ties, etc.

As part of some inspection schemes, there is also a roof inspection to ensure the trusses are done to specification and that the roofing and fixing details are correct. After this comes the pre-plaster inspection, which is performed when the pipes and wires are in place but initially left exposed.

Once the windows are fitted, the building is at the 'first fix complete' stage, and ready for plaster boarding, or 'closing up the house'.

The last inspection for building regulations and warranties is known as the CML inspection to obtain the Council of Mortgage Lenders certificate. This entails checking everything as a completed product to ensure the building is ready and safe for occupancy, including access and use of the building.

The inspectors also verify that your fire regulations are complete and compliant by checking the alarms and ventilation systems, and that the isolators are in place for various services such as gas, electric, water, and relevant bodies. They confirm that the water board have fitted the metres and that they, the gas safe plumber, and the NICEIC-approved electrician have all signed off on the installations. They also perform a soil stack test to check whether the drainage holds water. Once they are satisfied with the results of all these inspections, they issue the CML certificate and building regulations are signed off.

This is fundamental because at this point, once it is declared fit for occupation, lenders will lend against the building. On our St James project, all eight of our properties were signed off for completion on a Friday. On the Saturday and Sunday, all eight tenants moved in.

With the build-to-rent strategy, this is fantastic as you can have zero voids from virtually day one. With the build-to-sell strategy, you must wait two or three weeks for the mortgage lenders to complete their paperwork and finalise the mortgage, assuming your purchaser has applied for a mortgage before moving in.

Whatever good things we build end up building us. – Jim Rohn

Secret Tip #12: Make sure all the communications and agreements you have with any contractor are written down and in the contract before commencing any works. Liaise with your solicitor to make sure you're covered for any uncertainties and eventualities.

Chapter 11 Property Development During the Crash

Since the start of the twentieth century, property development has fluctuated for many reasons. What is certain is that the UK needs homes to be built to continue to provide for its ever-increasing population.

In an article published by The Observer in 2014, the history of property development is explained over the various decades.[10] The author wrote that, in the 1920s, at 'the end of the first world war, Britain was a nation in which almost 80% of people rented their homes, almost all from private landlords'. The prime minister expressed concern at the state of available housing and introduced the 1919 Housing Act to subsidise building council houses for the soldiers coming home. It was 'the era of the three-bedroom semi and the expansion of cities out into the suburbs', and the availability of cheap money, thanks to low interest rates, caused housing to peak in the mid 1930s at 350,000 new builds a year.

In the 1940s, German bombers devastated much of the island's more populated areas, halting new construction. Money was tight, rationing was in full swing, and construction materials were understandably scarce as everything focused on the war effort. Those few council houses being built were now held to higher standards thanks to the insistence of the health and housing minister. Council house building took off in the post-war 1950s with the majority of it located 'beyond the newly created Green Belt surrounding London'.

The 1960s continued the building boom, but, according to the

10   Larry Elliott, 'A brief history of British housing', The Observer, 24 May 2014, https://www.theguardian.com/business/2014/may/24/history-british-housing-decade.

article, it was the age of 'the tower block, with quantity coming at the expense of quality', and that by the end of that decade, there were as many homeowner-occupied units as those with tenants.

The 1970s ushered in Britain's first housing bubble, during which average home prices increased more in three years than they had over the previous twenty years. The 1980s saw council tenants now being given the option to buy their units, sparking Britain's second housing bubble, which burst in the 1990s. Interest rates shot up to 15% or more as unemployment doubled to three million. Homes were repossessed in record numbers as house prices continued to fall. But by the end of the 1990s, things started to turn around, with developers seeking to meet the demand of the millennium's rising population, and the UK's third housing bubble began to inflate.

In 2007/2008, the global financial crisis brought things to a screeching halt and homebuilding fell precipitously to 1930s' levels.

I spoke with a London-based, medium-sized Plc development company about how they survived the recession. In 2005, 2006, and early 2007, homes were selling like hotcakes, they said, and demand was relentless and increasing, so much so that this developer limited the number of sales to individuals to a maximum of two homes per person per development. The company mainly sold to the UK market, although there were a growing number of Irish investors. Many buyers were speculatively purchasing properties before the recession, planning to 'flip' them – that is, to take profit on contracts without legally completing.

This is a common trend just before a recession or cooling of the market. A sudden spike in property sales leads to lender nervousness and probable down-valuations.

Before the recession, buy-to-let mortgage providers were offering 85% loan-to-value products. Some even offered 90%. The demand rose so high at one point that in order to spread risk and prevent investors from taking too much of the stock, which they might then fail to mortgage and complete on, the company limited the property sales to one property per person per development. The remaining difficulty was that buyers could re-market the units pre-completion, with no control on mark-up, with assignees having valuation problems because price levels varied wildly within the same development.

The development company I spoke to was watching the market closely, with concern, as workers were filmed walking out of Lehman Brothers carrying cardboard boxes packed with their personal belongings. A global financial firm had been bankrupted in the financial crisis, with no bailout offered. It was unprecedented.

This development company, however, had built up good working relationships with its development financing banks and with the HBOS group, and had kept its lenders openly informed of everything they were doing in the preceding good years, including inviting them all to see the quality of the work being produced and sharing all pricing information. They had employed a net pricing strategy throughout: no hidden incentives and no inflating for discounts.

Because of this, the lenders supported the company's valuations as far as they possibly could, until 2009.

The recession

'The recession was like jumping into a swimming pool and not knowing how deep it was', one of them told me. 'You couldn't see the bottom.' Property prices spiralled downward. Lenders had tightened their lending, dropped their loan-to-value to 65 or 70%, which meant a lot of the speculative buyers were no longer able to legally complete.

Buyers were split among three categories: 1) Those who purchased with a long-term vision, contingency funds, and could afford to proceed; they would just have to put up more of a deposit to purchase; 2) Those who could afford to buy but wanted to pull out of the contract anyway, in which case the company took them to the High Court for breach of contract and obtained favourable judgment in all cases; and 3) Those who simply could no longer afford to buy, as they couldn't afford to increase their deposit (about 10–15% of all sales).

In the latter instance, the company took the 10% non-refundable deposit and set out to re-sell the properties. Through controlled, orderly re-marketing, they succeeded in re-selling at around 90% of the market value before the crash. As they had secured the earlier 10% deposit, they didn't lose much beyond the extra time required to re-sell.

Some of the big developers looked into the build-to-rent market, hoping to try to hold on to their stock and rent instead of sell the properties at a discount. There was certainly an increase in would-be tenants as a result of the recession, but the development finance lenders of these developers would be looking to call in the loans upon build completion. So, instead, many developers focused on building properties for housing associations instead of outright sale homes and waited for the open market to slowly recover.

Listed developers' share prices dropped dramatically, as much as 25% overnight in some cases and by about 90% over the space of a few months. These were indeed scary times for developers.

After the first quarter of 2010, the London market showed signs of recovering. Development finance banks were asking for more properties to be sold off-plan before they would advance development funding, so this London-based developer I spoke to doubled their required deposit amount and started looking for investors further afield. Investors from Hong Kong, Singapore, and Malaysia were a lot more liquid and could afford to pay the higher deposits, which in turn increased the development lenders' confidence to continue lending.

Properties were being sold almost two years in advance, with a 10% deposit taken on exchange and a further 10% a year later, providing greater completion security, backed by the developer's strong reputation and excellent customer satisfaction results. Gradually, owner-occupiers returned to the market and the company survived the recession, having learned much.

What's next for property development

What lies ahead? Where do we see property development going? What's happening with the market? And when might be the next crash?

Nobody knows. No-one can predict exactly what might happen, or when. However, it's safe to say that it's not a question of if – it is a question of when.

That said, economic analysts and property experts can make a few assumptions. Growth of property transactions and prices in the UK has slowed down since the Brexit vote, from which the outcome is still uncertain at the time of this writing, but demand for homes should continue to increase, as should house prices in all regions of the UK, according to the UK's biggest estate agency group, Countrywide.

Part of me thinks that estate agents say that to protect themselves. A report by Business Insider, issued just four days after the Countrywide report, suggests that Morgan Stanley, a global leading financial services firm, predicts a fall – a correction – in house prices of 1.6% in 2018. The fact that it is cited as a correction suggests to me that the prices will likely increase again once the economy stabilises.

Property will always be speculative. No one can predict what will happen. One thing is for sure, however: The best way to avoid losing any money in real estate is to do nothing. But there does remain a demand for homes. Everyone has to live somewhere.

The Government are promoting the need for more homes, as published in its housing white paper in February 2017,[11] and appear to be backing smaller developers and favouring the private rental sector (PRS) and build-to-rent schemes.

We will continue to build, but we will always have a precautionary view of our GDV, our gross development value, to provide something of a fall-back should property prices drop. We want to predict the drop and work our figures out on the lower end of our GDV.

If, by the end of the development, property prices haven't fallen, then everything above our predicted GDV is profit, assuming we haven't overspent on our build costs, which we are always careful to over-estimate. At 25% profit, we have a lot of contingencies in place. We have allowed for the possibility of prices dropping. And if build costs increase, we have allowed for that as well. Profit might, in a drop, reduce to 20%, or even 15%.

But even that is still profit.

---

11   See https://www.gov.uk/government/collections/housing-white-paper.

If opportunity doesn't knock, build a door. – Milton Berle

Secret Tip #13: Don't get sucked into analysis paralysis. Look at all your options and decide when the right time is to start. I just wished I had started years earlier. Property invariably goes up in value over the long term.

Chapter 12 Property Developments as a Secondary Strategy

Starting a property development for the first time understandably takes time – time, patience, and, more importantly, persistence.

On a good day, the highs are brilliant – you're ahead of schedule, under budget, and the site is humming along. On the low days, you've overspent, you've had a break-in, the copper pipes have been stolen, and someone has carved the words 'I am the devil man' in your newly hung composite door. (Certainly, you think, no one could accuse the perpetrator of a lack of self-awareness.)

Things will go wrong, and they will need your attention. Even highly experienced major developers have challenges. I know, because I used to work for them. Even from my place in the sales office, I was dealing with onsite problems (although nothing to do with the construction side, as I can't even put up a shelf.)

You must always stay on top of what is happening onsite, to keep a watchful eye on the entire project. If this is your first development, I would suggest you try not to focus on anything else that might distract you from the details of your development. We were the same when we started. Andi focused most of his time and energy on St James while my primary focus was on finding HMO properties to generate a cash flow strategy for us.

I found our first small HMO in Kettering, in July/August 2014. We completed on the property in September, with help from my nan, who invested some money via a loan agreement into the project. (My nan really has been hugely supportive of what we are doing, to help me grow the business she knew I had always wanted. Considering how she looked after me when I was a young boy and took such good care of my grandad while he was alive, it's wonderful to be able to return the favour now and pay her interest on the loan she made to us. I would like to take this opportunity to thank her for her help. We certainly wouldn't be here without her. She's helped and supported us constantly through the initial stages of growing our business. The same goes to every single one of our previous investors – you know who you are. You are one of the key reasons we can grow and develop, so thank you.)

The property we purchased was a small 3-bed terraced house in Kettering, with the intent to convert it into a 4-bed HMO which would rent at £500 per month, per room. The going rate in Kettering at the time was about £425 per month, per room, but we were going very high quality – I would have happily lived there – and so I felt I could push the price up.

In September, when we completed the purchase of that property, I handed in my notice to my employer. I had one month's gardening leave, which gave me a month's income before I'd feel the pinch of no steady income. I was faced with a challenge. I had to make sure the house conversion was finished and fully rented within that month before my income ground to a halt.

That was a huge step for me at the time. Sometimes, when you become successful, you forget what it was like to struggle at the start. I faced the very real likelihood of going months without any income, especially as our units were priced above market. And my wife and I had a child on the way. I had to make it work. But I felt reasonably confident I could get it done whilst Andi concentrated on St James. Surely four weeks would be plenty of time to convert a house into four HMO rooms, wouldn't it?

It took about eight weeks in total. I learnt a lot in those eight weeks. I learnt that I hate stripping wallpaper. (Does anyone enjoy it, I wonder?) I discovered that sanding paint off architrave is mind-numbingly tedious. I discovered that watching paint dry is just as exciting as it's reputed to be. I discovered that converting a house is hard work, and invariably takes longer than you think. I discovered that there is a lot more that goes into a house than I'd realised.

The most important thing I discovered during those stressful eight weeks was that I did not want to ever do it again. Ever!

We advertised the property for room rents and we had our first viewings booked in. I met with two interested parties at the property and showed them around, detailing the extent of the conversion, with which I was intimately familiar with, naturally. They each took a rental for £500 a month. Brilliant. We had our first income.

The other two units didn't take long to let either because the house was virtually brand new and we had converted it to a very nice standard which we were proud of.

This standard would become our norm. White walls. Dark-grey carpets. Metro grey tiles in the kitchens. A lot of the properties that we do today, whether they are new-build or conversion, all have the same wall and carpet colours, tiles, kitchens, bathroom fittings, and so on. It is easier and more efficient that way, as our build team know just what we want and what to get.

This HMO was bringing in a gross monthly rental income of £2,000, with about £700 worth of monthly expenses, giving us a net monthly income of £1,300. It wasn't quite what I needed to cover my previous income, but it wasn't too far off.

Andi and I agreed that I would take all of the rental income for the time being to cover my living expenses as that would allow me to focus all my time on property, rather than just evenings and weekends. The HMO was running well, fully occupied, and it has stayed pretty much the same ever since. We have since re-mortgaged it, releasing my nan's money to her, with interest.

She promptly reinvested with us, and why wouldn't she? We'd just given her around five times what she would have received had she left it in the bank. That's before we take inflation into account.

This illustrated that although we were doing a development at St James, it didn't prevent us from buying, converting, and completing other small projects at the same time, since there were two of us working together. Andi continued to focus on the development whilst I focused on buying other smaller properties to boost our cash flow.

The first time you do something like a development or HMO conversion, it's tough, no question, especially as it's all new to you. But the time you invest and your persistence will lead to bigger and better things, if you keep that forward momentum going.

Because of the HMO we did, we picked up a few more investors who could see and were interested in what we were doing. It is very much a compound effect. One of Andi's contacts expressed an interest in getting into property, having seen what we were doing, so we agreed to joint venture the next HMO with him. He would invest the money to purchase and convert, and for that he would receive 50% of the net rental income once completed. He was a successful businessman who understood the model and was very impressed by our first conversion.

In March 2015, I found us a property and we purchased it for £99,000. We spent about £50,000 converting it into a 5-bed HMO, again each unit earning us about £500 per month, and then had it re-valued at £200,000 and mortgaged 75% of it. That released the £149,000 out of pocket for the purchase and refurb, added another successful property to our portfolio, and delighted yet another investor.

The old Kettering shoe factory

During the conversion of our second HMO, which I didn't get involved in, I found a property that hadn't sold at auction, which was so lovely that I was baffled as to why it hadn't sold. It was an old shoe factory in the centre of Kettering. The building was three storeys high, with exquisitely detailed brickwork around the windows. It was built in 1873 specifically for the shoe industry, which in Northamptonshire at the time was massive.

Because I was born in Northampton, I have a passion for good quality shoes and I love the Northamptonshire brands: Church's, Loakes, Bakers, and particularly Jeffery-West, of which I have a small collection. (If anyone reading this knows the owners of Jeffrey-West, a few more pairs in my wardrobe wouldn't go amiss.) My stepdad's grandad once said to me, 'There are only two things in life worth investing in: quality shoes and a decent mattress, because if you're not in one, you're in the other'.

I'd make that three things: quality shoes, a decent mattress, and property, because if you're not in one, you're in the other, and the last could make you a shitload of money. (Needs work, I know.)

Maybe it was my fascination for shoes that first piqued my interest in the building in Kettering. I sent our architect to have a look and he checked on English Heritage to see if it was listed and discovered it wasn't. However, after completing the purchase with the help of yet another new investor, our solicitor discovered that, contrary to what we had thought, the property was in fact a Grade II-listed building, but it was listed as on the street next to the one it was actually on, which is how we'd missed it.

This understandably put a spanner in the works. We were only buying the ground floor of the building – buying the leasehold. The two upper floors had previously been converted into eight flats, while the ground floor we had purchased was office space, with a use class designation of B1.

Under a permitted development consent, you can convert a 'B1 (a) (Office)' to a 'C3 (dwelling house)'. This had been our intention from the beginning, but now we would have to apply for planning consent to convert it.

To get consent to convert, we also needed consent from the freeholder. The freehold was with company receivers (similar to liquidators). They obviously had no desire to hold on to the freehold so I suggested to the solicitors that we purchase the freehold from the receivers for £1. They agreed, as long as we paid their associated legal fees.

Our plan for a quick in-and-out conversion was starting to look like a much longer process. We had completed the purchase in June and had hoped to have it completed in six months, by the end of 2015. That August, the planning committee refused our application for lack of amenity space and over-development. Using our free go, we reduced our plan of a six-bed to five and resubmitted the application, along with some other minor amendments.

To our relief, come December, the application for planning was approved the second time around, along with the consent for a listed building to be converted, but our initial plan had been to have already finished the conversion by this time. Instead, we hadn't even started.

Time onsite costs money. Luckily, there were enough margins in the deal to take all the money back out at the end of the project, and our investor was happy as he had still been earning money on his original investment.

From purchase to completion, the project took sixteen months versus six, at a total cost of about £225,000, and was now valued at £320,000. And all of this had taken place whilst we were still developing the Victoria Street site.

If we had not built in both a time and money contingency, we would have been in trouble. It is so important that you budget every deal you do to take longer than you expect, and factor that in from the beginning.

Blake Henderson Ltd

We met Paul in 2014, when we were just starting out. We were attending a three-day property seminar and Paul was attending a different real estate seminar adjacent to ours. We met at registration and kept bumping into him during the breaks.

Paul and his partner were based in Cumbria, where he ran his family's business which had been building and renovating for generations. At the time we first met him, Paul was already converting properties into HMOs, but for other people, not himself. He reached out to us later, after we had finished our St James development, surprised and impressed to learn that we had gone from our first buy-to-let property to 17 in a single year, the eight we built at St James, the four-bed HMO, the five-bed HMO, the factory five-bed HMO, a six-bed house we converted into three one-bed flats, and our two previous buy-to-lets. He wanted to know how we had done it.

At the time, he was converting houses for other people and had done nothing for himself. Andi invited Paul down for the weekend and, by the Sunday, had detailed what we had done, and how. Paul mentioned an opportunity in Cumbria that we decided to investigate, and it turned out that what he had described was an understatement. (Most people tend to exaggerate when describing anything they label an opportunity and inflate the figures. Paul had done the opposite. The figures were better than he had described.) The end result was that we formed a new SPV, a special purpose vehicle, which we called Blake Henderson Limited. We wanted a name that seemed old-fashioned, as the town was a working town but quite elegant. The name derives from the surnames of Andi's Grandma Blake and his wife's Gran Henderson.

The business of Blake Henderson was to create serviced apartments to help satisfy the demand for housing in Barrow-in-Furness for contract workers at BAE Systems, GlaxoSmithKline, DONG Energy, Siemens, Centrica and other big companies. Our target was one hundred rooms in a year, and so we started looking at feasible conversion sites and found several.

We used bridging finance, along with some private investment finance, to purchase three houses and three pubs in three days. By November 2016, we supported a total of seven bridging loans, arranged by Kevin Wright of Positive Property Finance, to purchase seven properties, six for this project and another for a separate property in Northampton.

When you purchase six properties in three days you get noticed. The council were initially nervous, but soon supported us when Andi outlined the quality of what we intended to create when we applied for planning. The houses were a four-bed, a five-bed and a six-bed, while the pubs were 13-, 17-, and 31-bed properties, and we subsequently purchased an additional six-bed property. That put us short of our 100-room target by just 18 rooms, which wasn't too bad. (We are actually in the process now of converting an old solicitors' office into 18 flats, so our target of 100 rooms will be accomplished soon enough.) The properties took longer than 12 months to obtain planning and convert, but we managed to create 82 rooms.

It wasn't as simple as it sounds though. With six bridging loans on the properties in Barrow, we had to secure quite a lot of private finance, and there was considerable paperwork to fill out. We also had a close brush with the law.

I had gone up to Barrow for my first look at the properties on which our offers had been accepted, before we completed the sales on the pubs. Andi, Paul and I collected the keys from the various estate agents and went to see the biggest of the three pubs, the one we intended to convert into 31 rooms.

We unlocked the door and had a look around. The pub, a three-storey building, had evidently been closed down for quite some time. We went to take a look upstairs but found the door that led to the stairway locked. We had been given a ring with literally dozens of keys on it and spent about 45 minutes trying – and failing – to find the right key. We had come a long way to only be able to look at the ground floor. There was a second door, this one from the outside, which was also locked, leading to the courtyard at the back, where another upstairs access lay.

Paul went to have a look in the basement and discovered it had access to the courtyard out the back, but the door leading upstairs was also locked, and we didn't have the key.

When I looked around, Paul had disappeared again. This time he had decided to climb the external fire exit that went up to the top floor. The upper half of the fire door was glass, and the putty was cracked, and so the glass came out quite easily.

Andi and I followed Paul up the fire escape, wishing we hadn't had to wear suits for our meetings that day, and following Paul's example, threw a leg over the bottom half of the door and climbed through, brushing the dust off our dark trousers. As it turned out, our actions had not gone unnoticed below by the customers of the cash machine opposite the pub.

'There's a policeman in the garden', Andi observed, moments later. Paul and I peered out the window. Indeed, there were three police cars flanking the pub and an officer stood below, signalling us to come down.

It flashed through my mind that only five minutes had passed since we'd broken through the door, and I was pleased to see the police response time was tip-top here. We opened the front door and half a dozen police officers walked in.

We quickly explained the situation, that we were purchasing the building and had the owner's consent, and keys, to look around. They hesitated, looking us up and down. I was now grateful we were dressed well, and a quick check on the radio confirmed our story. They examined our IDs and one of the officers asked what we planned to do with the building. They were intrigued when we outlined our plans. Good, I thought. We had police approval too.

'I did think you were some of the smartest-dressed robbers we'd ever seen', one officer commented, as we all filed out.

They waited as Andi locked the front door.

Andi has been taking monthly trips up to Barrow to keep an eye on the project, while I turn my attention to other aspects of our business. That's the beauty of a partnership.

An aside on Barrow-in-Furness

If you have never been to Barrow-in-Furness in Cumbria, it has just one road in and out, and is miles from anywhere, and certainly a long way from Northampton. Shortly after we started on the project, our mentor, Mark Homer, expressed interest in seeing what we were doing in Barrow, as it was not a typical development.

Mark has a licence to pilot private helicopters, so we took a Robinson R44 up to Barrow, which took about an hour and twenty minutes, saving us what would otherwise be a four-hour drive. The day was lovely and we could see for miles. I used Facebook Live to film part of the trip, which took us over the Pennines. We landed the helicopter at Abbey House Hotel, a gorgeous building set in fourteen acres of landscaped gardens, built for the Vickers Shipyards to home Commander Craven in 1914.

Andi and I showed Mark around the town, including our properties. Near the end of our lunch, in the hotel, the skies clouded over and it started to drizzle. We hurried back to the helicopter.

The clouds were so low that we had to avoid the Pennines, because ours was a visually guided helicopter, rather than an instrument-guided one, and flew instead along the M6 south. The rain fell, harder and harder. Not only did we not have instrument navigation, I discovered; we also did not have windscreen wipers. Eventually, we were forced to land in a field just north of Warrington, where we waited an hour for the skies to clear slightly.

By now, it was about 16:30, and there were still considerable low-hanging clouds, so we had to veer beyond a direct route, which drained the fuel tank, forcing us to land again, this time five hundred metres from Twycross Zoo.

The owner of the helicopter was Mark's instructor, and so he was a bit nonplussed to see us, having left in his chopper, return to the airfield in the back of a taxi. He was even more taken aback when Mark explained that the owner would have to be the one to retrieve his helicopter because Mark didn't have time. He would be busy delivering a keynote speech the next day.

My point in sharing this story is simply to remind you that no matter how experienced you are, you do not have complete control of everything. With a development, external factors beyond your control might force you to change your plans, and you may have to be flexible, to take more extraordinary measures to get to the finish. You only truly fail when you stop.

Secondary strategy success

Property development can be successful as a secondary strategy. These days, while Andi focuses on developments, I spend more time working with and training our students, yet he and I still confer on property deals, whether they are developments, commercial projects, or HMOs.

If you want to approach developments as a secondary strategy, the one thing you must always do is engage a project manager as part of your team, particularly if you are new to property development. It is critical that you are aware at all times of both what you need to do in the present moment and in the future. A project manager will handle that for you and keep you apprised.

A project manager is worth the cost to your development finance budget. The price you pay them shouldn't matter, as long as they do their job well enough and save you more than they cost. Their job is to make sure materials are bought at a good price and keep the project running smoothly, on time and on budget, because, again, time onsite costs money, and an inefficiently run project is going to be a costly one. If they charge, say, £45,000, then it is not unreasonable to expect them to bring the project in on time and on budget in a safe but cost-efficient way that saves you at least that £45,000.

Consider incentivising them, something that Andi and I have done in the past. We set a reasonable budget that makes the deal work. The budget includes the contingencies we insist on building in, but we incentivise our team by saying that we will give them half of what they responsibly save on the budget as a bonus.

So, if the budget is £700,000 and they bring in the deal at £670,000 total spend, half of that £30,000 saved is distributed amongst the individuals directly responsible for the savings, normally two to three members of our team. This motivates them to be efficient and save money on the job, as they will pocket some of that savings, and by incentivising them, we are likely pocketing a bit more than we might otherwise have done. Now, if they save £30,000 on materials but blow all or most if it because the project stretches beyond the anticipated time to complete, then there's no bonus. The idea is to encourage them to keep the project both under budget and within time.

We are not perfect and we will never be perfect. In the relatively short time since we started, we have made our share of mistakes. It's par for the course. What's important is that we have learnt from them. We have adapted the way we work to ensure we don't repeat our mistakes.

Richard Branson famously said, 'I have always believed that there is no point in having regrets, as you learn far more from mistakes than successes. Embrace a mistake and learn from it; don't regret them.'

I share his belief. We have been asked if we could go back and start again, would we change anything and, if so, what. I can honestly answer: nothing. I can't think of a single thing I would want to change since starting the business. I love what we do, and I'm enjoying where the business is going.

We wouldn't be where we are without educating ourselves both mentally and physically. By that I mean that we learnt about property investing and decided to get into developments, something that virtually nobody we knew was doing. We certainly didn't know of any courses that we could attend to learn the underlying theory and best practices.

What we did do was get out there and just do it, to take those first tottering steps on our way to what has turned out to be an unbelievably rewarding destination. Who knew?

I guess you could say that this is the real theme of this book, that getting out there and doing it is the best way to learn. Practical application of classroom theory in real-world situations.

It's a bit like learning to drive a car, as I mentioned at the start of chapter 5. You can study all the rules of the road, memorise what each road sign means, and understand intellectually what you have to do in order to pass the written test and operate a car. But it's only once you get behind the wheel that you start to appreciate all the intricacies involved, and how much risk is associated with every turn of the wheel, every tap of the brake or accelerator.

It's a tremendous responsibility. It's also incredibly exhilarating once you develop a little confidence and can relax and enjoy the feeling of sudden unlimited freedom.

We could teach you the art of a perfect development over a period of weeks or months and yet, as soon as you do a development for yourself, that's when you truly discover what a development involves, and how the risk/reward ratio really translates for you.

Accept that you will make mistakes. Everyone does. And learn from them.

A lesson we've never forgotten

One mistake we made early on concerned a development we were looking at towards the end of December 2014.

We were working on the St James project, in Northampton, when a development site three hundred metres up the road came onto the market. The site was a derelict bakery site which Google indicated had previously been a pharmaceutical factory or plant nursery that had remained derelict for years. It was right next to a park, and in an ideal location considering we were working just down the road.

What we didn't do was look too carefully at it, as the planning involved demolishing the existing building and constructing a six-storey, 44-unit scheme. This was way beyond what we had ever done. Our experience was still quite limited. We were still building our first project, so we dismissed it and concentrated on completing St James.

It was halfway into the build of our Victoria Street site, and after we had completed and refinanced the St James site, that the bakery site appeared again. This time, we were more prepared. We had been focusing on deals with GDVs of £1 million, whereas this one looked to be more like £6 million. It's nothing more than a multiple of six I told myself. It felt like a solid, if ambitious next step for us.

We crunched the numbers and did the due diligence. Because we had just completed the St James deal down the road, our research and knowledge of the area was spot-on, and we knew precisely how much the market value would be. It appeared to us that it could garner £1.8 million profit. That was a life-changing amount.

Andi and I went over it and over it. Was it right for us? Were our calculations correct? Could we manage it? Most importantly, could we find the finance?

We spoke to a few development finance lenders who were keen to lend and prepared to give us as much as 81% of the total costs, about £3.4 million. We would have to find the rest. We would simply have to consider giving a bit more away in order to find bigger sums of money.

We decided to make an offer, just shy of £1 million. The site was to build 44 units with no affordable houses and only £26,000 of Section 106 payments to be made, which was reduced from the original £260,000 by the vendors. We met with the landowners and they accepted our offer. We shook hands and verbally agreed to a deal granting us exclusivity for about two or three months to give us time to secure the finances needed to complete the deal.

We spoke to the development finance lender in preparation to complete on the deal and began applying for the finance. We had a valuation performed on the site, which cost us around £5,000 due to the size of the project, and it confirmed that our earlier calculations were correct.

Now that the finances were set, all we needed to do now was to find sufficient private investor finance to round out the deal. We incurred some additional costs in the process and eventually had some traction with funds.

We were now at the two-month mark. That's when we reached out to the vendors to discuss the completion of the deal.

Nothing. They didn't answer our calls. We kept ringing but there was no answer. It was fine, we told ourselves, confident that they couldn't have sold it to anyone else. After all, we had an exclusivity agreement on the site.

One day we called from a different number and the vendors picked up, not realising it was us. They admitted they had received a more attractive offer from another party. We went back to the drawing board to see if we could justify paying a higher price for the site.

A few days later, our solicitor phoned to say that the vendors had asked them to return any paperwork as they were no longer selling the site. This was devastating as the amount of time and effort we had spent on the site was considerable. We had also spent over £15,000 so far on the deal to get it to this point. And now we were about to lose that £15,000.

We thought we had exclusivity. We didn't. We had a handshake, a gentleman's bargain. But in this day and age, a handshake is not a legally binding contract. We were screwed.

It set us back a bit. We didn't have a plan B. We didn't have any other deals to move on to. We had put all of our eggs into one basket. I had spoken to people about our next deal.

After that experience, that lesson learned, we always ensure we have a few deals going at the same time, so we haven't got our eggs all in one basket. We always have a plan B, an exit strategy, and we get a legally binding exclusivity on deals now.

Recently, we agreed on a deal and exchanged contracts with a 10% deposit that is fully refundable if planning is not granted. We learnt a lot from that bakery deal. But we didn't let the loss of £15,000 get us down or deter us. That, we decided, was the cost of our education.

What it taught us was that we could do bigger deals. We could raise bigger sums of money. We could obtain finance for bigger projects. We learnt – irrevocably – the importance of a legally binding agreement.

One thing is for sure – it made us think bigger. The benefit of that, as Richard Branson would put it, was what we learned. We embraced it and learnt from it, instead of moaning about it or letting it deter us from continuing.

I'm telling you, we wouldn't change anything we'd done in the past. It's all been profitable.

Exclusivity – how to use it to protect yourself

So, what forms of exclusivity can you employ to ensure that something like what happened to us doesn't happen to you? There are a few different ways you can temporarily secure a plot of land you are negotiating on.

Lock-out agreement

A lock-out agreement is a short-term agreement between a potential buyer and seller that legally prevents the seller negotiating with any other party during the designated lock-out period while the buyer performs the necessary due diligence before proceeding with a purchase.

Lock-out agreements must meet certain criteria to be enforceable. If the seller breaches the agreement by selling to another party within the lock-out period, the buyer can claim only limited damages, sufficient to compensate them for their actual wasted time.

The lock-out agreement does not legally commit the seller to sell to the other party of the agreement any more than it compels the buyer to buy. The lock-out agreement is usually undertaken at the potential buyer's expense and registered with a solicitor.

The agreement should state an exact date or duration as to when the agreement expires and it is only a short-term agreement. If the buyer is looking for a longer-term agreement, an 'option to buy' might be a better solution.

Option to buy agreement

An option to buy is, as the name states, an agreement between the potential buyer and the seller, giving the buyer first option to buy. As with the lock-out agreement, an option to buy agreement is not a conditional contract, whereupon the buyer is obliged to purchase the property. An option to buy governs an offer to purchase subject to certain conditions, such as obtaining planning permission, within a designated period of time, potentially up to 21 years, at which point the buyer serves notice on the seller to sell the land. Option agreements are normally registered with the Land Registry, so a quick search there on a plot of land will reveal potentially interested parties of any superseding agreements that may exist.

Maximising value or rent

If you really love oranges, you want to squeeze out as much juice as possible. We love property, and we want to make sure we get the most out of it. We want to ensure we get the best and highest site valuation possible. We want the rent we charge to reflect the quality of property we provide. Ours are new-build properties, targeting young people looking for their first home, small families, and professionals.

We want our property to be quality, one we ourselves would happily live in. We are not in this business to squeeze out every penny of profit to the detriment of our tenants. We want our tenants – our customers – to enjoy living in our properties.

This sometimes means we need to spend a bit more than normal on a project in order for it to meet our standards and we're okay with that. Whilst ours are not high-end properties, they are well-built, well-equipped, quality rental units.

Creating a show home

When we are close to finishing a property development site, we create a show home, just like the big house builders do, even though we are building to rent, and not selling. We want the show unit to illustrate the property's full potential, so the potential tenants can see how it might ideally look. Some people can't visualise what a property will look like, once complete. Standing in an empty room, they struggle to picture even where the beds should go.

One benefit of creating a show home is that it can support the increased rent you can ask for. In St James, Northampton, the average monthly rent for a two-bed house was roughly £625. On our eight houses, that would be £5,000 a month, or £60,000 a year. Instead, we were able to ask for more rent and justify it by providing a show home to demonstrate its superiority over the average.

New-build properties for sale are generally priced at a premium because they are new. So why can't new-build rental properties demand a premium rent?

We asked for £795 per month for our eight St James units, and they all went, and we let the show home, with furniture included, for £850 a month. Instead of that £5,000 average monthly income, we earned £6,415, nearly £17,000 more a year. (That was about my wage when I left my job to start the business). That gets multiplied by the number of properties you have.

We had a very similar scenario with another eleven houses we built. I stood in one of the properties with a letting agent who advised we wouldn't get anymore than £600 for a two-bed. I explained what we had accomplished on our previous site, commanding above-average rents for what, I reminded him, were new-build rental properties, which aren't common. I asked him to advertise them for £750 instead. Five of the eleven went in the first week of advertising. Eleven houses at £600 is £6,600 per month, £79,200 a year. Instead, we got £750 a month for the nine unfurnished houses and £800 a month for the two show homes, one for each of the two styles we were offering. The rent per month was £8,450, not £6,600, which equates to £101,400 per year. That's a £22,200 difference.

Add this extra to that which we achieved on the St James property and it yielded us £39,180 of extra annual income. And the properties have been let ever since. Yes, our tenants could have chosen a less expensive rental elsewhere, but they preferred the higher quality standard of our property and were willing to pay a higher rent to get it.

Andi teases me about my ability to 'fluff a cushion', since I'm responsible for furnishing the show homes, but I always remind him that whilst pretty much anyone can build a picture frame, not everyone chooses well what to frame inside it!

Choose your show home carefully. It should be easily accessible from the road or a section of the site. And as it encourages potential tenants to walk over the site, it needs to be one of the better plots. For example, you would choose an end-terraced unit as opposed to a mid-terraced property, and it should be one of the larger ones, if you had varying numbers of bedrooms.

And it should be one of the first properties you complete. The sooner you can release a show home, the sooner you can line up tenants. Tenants generally must provide a month's notice to their current landlords, so many tenants are willing to take a property about a month before you've completed it, as long as they can see by way of the show home what it's going to look like. That said, you will still get the odd tenant who will reserve earlier and is willing to wait for the property to be finished. With sale properties, you can start selling other plots on the site before the foundations have even been dug.

Refinancing your build-to-rent development

Congratulations. You've just completed your development. You're done. Well, almost. The final part of the build-to-rent strategy is to refinance or re-mortgage the development, something you will have ideally begun to work on two to three months before completion.

Let's use our Victoria Street development as an example and run through the process of re-mortgaging your build-to-rent development. Size is a factor in negotiating financing, but you will have already spoken to your commercial finance broker at the beginning of your development and likely identified which lender(s) are your best choice, although that can change, depending on current rates and terms. But you should have an idea of what rate to expect.

Ask your commercial finance broker to provide you with at least five sets of terms from various lenders. You may want to fix your interest rate for two, three, or five years. There are even some 10-year-fixed products, but most carry early redemption penalties, so if you had to re-mortgage or sell before the early redemption period expired, you would incur additional costs. (Most of our mortgages are variable interest rate loans.)

Next, you must decide whether you want an interest-only mortgage versus a capital repayment mortgage. With a capital repayment mortgage, you pay the interest on the mortgage each month plus some of the principal debt. A 25-year term loan means that at the end of those 25 years, you will have paid off the principal and interest due entirely. You can make over- (excess) payments in order to accelerate the date on which you will have satisfied the mortgage, but payments of additional principal are capped each year as to how much you can pay.

An interest-only mortgage is one where your payment covers only the monthly interest incurred, making your monthly payments lower than those of a capital repayment mortgage, but at the end of the term of the loan, you must repay the full loan amount still due, having only paid the interest to date.

Decide what is more important to you, a higher cash flow per month, in which case you might prefer the interest-only product, or paying down the debt, normally a higher payment per month, thus reducing your net monthly cash flow.

Financing a development with a long-term interest-only mortgage can be attractive in that if you intend to hold the property long term, as property prices increase, which they generally do over an extended period of time, along with inflation and the site's capital appreciation, it will naturally reduce the loan-to-value ratio, the mortgage amount against the gross development value, even without having paid down any of the principal debt.

Victoria Street was valued at just over £1,684,000, an average of about £153,000 per property, whereas the mortgage was £1,061,346. Dividing the mortgage amount by the GDV gives a loan-to-value of 63%. If the site were to increase in value by 20% over a number of years, bringing the GDV up to £,2,020,800, dividing the £1,061,346 mortgage by that would bring the loan-to-value ratio down to just 52%.

If we look at it in the very distant future, say, in fifty years' time, and the site is now hypothetically worth £10 million and still carries an interest-only mortgage of just over £1 million, the loan-to-value would drop to 11%. With inflation, the face value of the loan might be such that the entire sum could be quite manageably afforded, even payable in one lump sum. After all, today's £1,061,346 was equivalent to just £62,027 fifty years ago.

So, the process of re-mortgaging your site should start around about two to three months before you're scheduled to complete. Just like with a residential mortgage, your lender will require certain information from you, starting with:

Your name

The property address

Details and type of property (commercial, semi commercial or residential; most likely, yours would be residential)

Purchase price

Market value

Length of time the mortgage is needed

Tenancies in place, length, and gross and net operating (rental) income

Details of portfolio

Once the lender finishes reviewing these documents, you might still be about a month and a half from completing the site. The lender will instruct a valuation which must take place before they can offer a mortgage amount, something that ideally will happen after you have already let all of the properties on assured shorthold tenancy (AST) agreements, one per rental unit. The reason is because the mortgage is calculated based on the rental value of the entire site, something lenders call stress testing.

If your site is under an SPV, the lender will stress test at around

125% of your net rental income based on a mortgage interest rate of about what is currently 5–6% (see "Build-to-rent strategy" in chapter 3). If the net rental income comfortably exceeds the mortgage payments, then you should be okay. This shows the lender that were interest rate to rise, you could still cover the mortgage amount.

The valuation may take place before the units are finished, but the valuer (property appraiser) will need to enter every single property, so the units need to be at an almost-complete stage. If the value comes to the site and is unable to access every property, you may have to pay for them to return. The valuer may also wish to return to the site one final time, having previously accessed every unit, to complete the valuation, something the lender may insist upon.

Once the valuation comes back, your mortgage broker sends you the offer, which determines at what level you can mortgage your development. This is where knowing the purchase price, cost of build, interest on the development finance, legal fees, professional fees, and costs related to time spent onsite pays off. If your total spend is less than your mortgage value, then you've done it – completed a property development using none of your own money. With thorough due diligence, underestimation of the gross development value, and overestimation of the build costs, you will reap the rewards of your development. On our Victoria Street project, our total spend was around £1,045,000. The mortgage totalled £1,061,346, and the gross development value was £1,684,000. That is a potential profit of £639,000, £622,654 of it being equity.

Our commercial finance broker is a company called Pilotfish Partnership, based in Peterborough, which sort out our development and re-mortgage finance.

Selling your property development

If you have adopted the build-to-sell method, hopefully you have sold all of the plots before they were completed. To do this, you need to start advertising as soon as possible. The size of your development will determine which route is best to take.

Once you have started onsite, let everyone know what you are developing. Create advertising boards on your site. Get some 3D images created for your development, like we did with our coloured-box concept. As mentioned earlier, you can get these images done quite easily on websites such as fiverr.com or their equivalent.

Once you have 3D images of the development site, get someone to design the advertising board for you. Look at similar advertising boards from the big developers and advertise your developments in a similar fashion: 2, 3 & 4 bed luxury homes for sale, expected springtime. Don't list a specific month, as you may need flexibility should you go over the time expected to build.

Once you have the advertising boards, put someone in charge of answering the phone or responding to buyer inquiries by email. This is something you could outsource to an estate agent, to have them do the marketing for you. I would look to pay them anywhere between one and two per cent of the sales fee to field the enquiries.

Consider suggesting to all potential buyers that they use your commercial finance broker for their mortgages. After all, they are your power team and the more you look after them, the better they will look after you. And if they do a great job for you, you can recommend them enthusiastically to your customers, a win-win–win situation.

We love the idea of the law of reciprocity, that when you make a nice gesture to someone and expect nothing back in return, the chances are that they will reciprocate the gesture in some way, sometimes even exceeding the initial gesture. (And sometimes extend the same level of generosity to someone else, as well, in a ripple effect.) That's one reason why we have listed all of our terrific team members at the back of this book, because they're worth every penny we pay them. The other reason is to help you find quality providers with a proven track record.

The more you can help someone else, the better. And another advantage of having them use your broker is that you can more easily track the progress of the application.

I would suggest you use no more than two estate agents to advertise the properties for you and let each of them know there is another agent selling the properties. This will generate sufficient healthy competition and galvanize a more spirited effort.

When you sell the properties, ask your agent to take a reservation fee, normally around £500–1000, to take the property off the market and then look to exchange contracts on the property 28 days from reservation. Completion will take place, assuming you have sold the property, about two weeks following the practical completion of the property and it has been signed off by building control.

I have always believed that there is no point in having regrets as you learn far more from mistakes than successes. Embrace a mistake and learn from it; don't regret them. –Richard Branson

Secret Tip #14: Plan your exit before you start. Speak to mortgage brokers before you commence work. Knowing what options you have at the beginning of the development will help you at the end. Don't limit yourself to the lenders available by not speaking to them first.

Chapter 13 How to Get Started

What does it take to get started?

What do you need?

How can I help you?

When I started, if you remember, I had no money. I had no development experience, I had no time, and I had no track record. So, what did I have to offer my new partner? Probably not a lot, to start with. But what I could do was research lenders, help identify and secure private investors, keep the investors in the loop by giving them updates, speak to the letting agents towards the end of the development, find HMO properties, find other development opportunities, and speak to brokers.

Some experienced developers don't like this side of the business, so, although you may not have experience, you can offer your efforts in this capacity to a partner with hard skills in development. This way, the one I have outlined in this book, is the new way of looking into developments. You've got to start somewhere.

Have you ever looked at a job advert that states 'Must have experience'? Have you ever questioned, as I have, how anyone is supposed to get experience when every job asks for someone who is already experienced?

It's the same for developments. You can start somewhere by adding a little bit to the development and learn on the job. I started with little experience outside of sales and some knowledge of home layouts. Andi had no money or actual development experience either – what he had was building/renovation experience, but no development experience. What we shared was the determination to do it and do it well.

Determination, however, is not enough. You still must possess a good grasp of how developments work. We had a site, which we could give developments a go on. We had each other to celebrate the highs with (which we did – when we completed the purchase of the 22-garage site in St James, we decided to have a drink for every garage that we had just purchased; I think we still have about seven left to drink) and we supported each other during the low days, working out solutions together (often also over a pint).

Andi's track record in building, even though it was mainly extensions, gave us credibility when it came to finding investors. Funding Circle accepted us based on Andi's track record, as did friends and family. We had enough to allow us to do our research and due diligence to start with.

I was still employed, so I didn't need to cover the costs of my time, which was spent working evenings and weekends. We had enough capital raised from private investors to cover the costs of our architect and professional and legal fees to start with.

We worked hard; we were persistent and consistent. We believed in ourselves and in each other. We knew that we were both doing as much as we could to help the business. I probably had more of a reason to devote myself to this than Andi, as he still had income from his company, Red Box Developments. I had to make it work.

When you're comfortable, it's hard sometimes to summon sufficient motivation to want to instigate this level of change. A decent salary, company car, pension, and private healthcare can stall even those who hate their job, because it's easier for them to give in to the inertia that comfort brings, whereas the ones who are motivated to change their lives, no matter what they do or don't have to lose, give it everything they have to make it work. They need a change.

So, tell me, do you want to give this your all? Are you prepared to face some challenges? Do you want to make some money or free up your time? Do you have a reason to start? What is your vision? Where do you see yourself in a few years' time? What will it take for you to start – to try, to give it a go?

How to get going

The first thing is to find out as much information as possible from people who already are involved in doing developments already. Since you're reading this book (and maybe you've taken one of our classes), you have already begun to educate yourself in the various aspects of the development process. It is critical that you understand the potential pitfalls and decide for yourself whether you can cope with the associated risks. Nothing rewarding, nothing worth doing, comes without some risk.

A good source of information can be found on our Facebook group, called Property Developers Secrets. Social media and networking can not only help educate you but help you to build your power team. It is also worth letting everyone know about what you do and what you are doing. This can be done by live videos, posts and comments, showing your challenges, giving advice, and ultimately attracting potential investors and future opportunities by being active and visible.

Decide whether you want to undertake this on your own, as part of a partnership, or as part of a larger team.

Decide where you want to invest.

Decide what exit strategy you want to adopt: build-to-rent or build-to-sell.

Have a clear idea of what your next 12 to 24 months will look like.

Focus on one development at a time, if it is your first development site, or you lack experience. Stick to a site with less than 10 houses or 1,000 square metres to start, if this is your first project.

Have the mind-set to achieve. 'You have to believe before you achieve', as they say. 'Stop dreaming of the life you'd love and start living the life that you dream' is what I say.

Start assembling your future power team and prepare them for the day you find a viable site.

Set up your SPV/special purpose vehicle and a bank account.

Start lining up your finance sources by talking to as many people as possible. A development is a business, so talk to people about potentially investing in your deal. I call this warming up your investors. Explain to people how the site works, how you will pay them back, and how they can invest. Ask them whether, based on a certain percentage or split, they would be interested in being told once a deal becomes available.

A lot of people will say yes at this point, as it doesn't require any commitment. It'll only be when you have a deal and ask them again that you can ascertain just how interested they are – if they truly meant it when they said yes. But you will have done the hard work; you will have broken the ice. They are warm and you can call them.

It's easier to ask for money when you have a theoretical deal rather than an actual deal, so speak to as many people as possible while you're still in the theoretical stage.

Line up the development finance.

Put in the necessary effort to find deals. (Revisit chapter 7 for our detailed suggestions.) Apply the 30/10 principle to 'traffic light' your possibilities and be disciplined about it. We're talking only one deal a day. Once you get into the swing of appraising deals, you will learn to do it quite quickly. Don't skip the full site appraisal if the deal stacks up though. Offer on sites at the value that you can justify paying in order for the project to be profitable, and not based on what the vendor wants. Be strict on this.

Don't chase a deal because you like it. Again, this is a business. Don't get overly invested emotionally. Have a Plan A, Plan B, and Plan C (the Armageddon Plan).

Launch

'You don't have to be great to start, but you have to start to be great', as Zig Ziglar says, remember. My other mentor, Rob Moore, talks about the 'Ready, fire, aim' approach, where you just do it now, and get perfect later. That, for me, is the best way to make a change.

Don't worry if you start and nothing comes for the first few months. It will eventually, if you persevere. Don't abandon ship. Keep going.

Keep educating yourself and set yourself a target. Have an aim for your first year. That goal should be what some call a stretch goal, not easily achievable but not wholly impossible either.

I recommend you read the book The 10X Rule, by Grant Cardone, who explains that setting a target 10 times greater than what you want to achieve, and taking actions that are 10 times what you feel is necessary to achieve is the only way to fulfil your true potential. He says that the biggest mistake people make in life is not setting high enough goals for themselves. The point is that by aiming for the 10X point, even if you only reach 20% of your target, that's still twice as much as you thought you could accomplish in the first place.

12-month target

Let's assume that your original goal was to build three houses in twelve months. Using the 10X rule, three becomes a new target of 30 houses in your first year. In looking at the diagram below, which represents the year that lies ahead, your starting point is zero, marked 'NOW' at the bottom of the diagram.

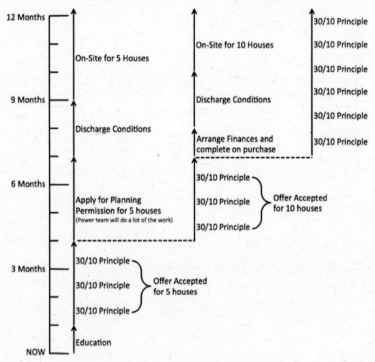

This is the start of your plan for the next 12 months.

Your first month is spent educating yourself, learning the process.

The next three months (months 2, 3, and 4) will be spent putting that education into practice. These three months will be spent appraising 90 deals, one deal each day, and putting in offers on 30 of them. One or more may get accepted. The rest remain in your pipeline.

Then it's time to apply for planning permission, which will take three months (months 5, 6, and 7). Assuming planning is granted, months 8 and 9 will be used to discharge some condition in preparation for your eventual planning acceptance and readying to start.

That's good. But, whilst the site was in for planning during months 5, 6, and 7, what if you were still appraising a site a day, and offering on 10 each month? If you were still calling all the offers you made in your previous months to see whether they were prepared to accept your offer yet?

Sure enough, another deal gets accepted, say, in month 7. This second site already has planning for 10 houses, so it's just a case of gathering the finances together and discharging the pre-commencement conditions (done in months 8 and 9).

So, now before the end of the year, you have two sites, one with planning for 10 houses and another pending planning for five. That's a total of 15 houses, 50% of your original 30-house target and 400% higher than your original goal of just three houses.

Yes, I know – you're thinking that being new to development, I suggest that you focus only on your first development site. That's fine. But if you continue to invest effort in simply finding sites, you can sell the additional ones you find, or develop them yourself afterwards. Or you might be comfortable with doing a couple of sites at the same time.

That is for you to decide. I don't want to hold you back if you would be comfortable doing more than one. If you are not comfortable and want to stick with the site for five houses until completion, that's perfectly acceptable – and still 66% more than your 3-house original goal. That alone could represent the difference between hundreds of thousands of pounds.

No track record?

Another thing that might hold you back from getting started is a lack of experience or track record. This is particularly important when you look to raise finance from a development lender. They need some assurance that you know what you're doing.

My suggestion is that, on your first development, you don't get too greedy regarding the end profit. Don't be afraid to give a bit more away as a way of investing in your own development career future. Don't hesitate to offer a slightly higher interest rate to a potential investor to get them interested to invest. Don't be afraid to involve someone else, someone with valuable skills, in the project. Just be careful who you choose, as you will be financially connected. Do your due diligence on the person(s) you involve, as this is as key as the due diligence involved in evaluating a deal.

One such person is the builder. If the builder agrees to be part of the deal, you can source and use their experience for your development. You can also use their track record to bolster yours and facilitate obtaining development finance. The right builder might be interested in becoming involved in the project, as the long-term return to them will exceed simply being contracted on the job. Just take Andi and me, for example. I had no money, track record, or time. I joint ventured with him and we started developing together. We both share the deals on a 50/50 split but we both drive and push each other to do bigger and better things.

Most lenders want to see someone with experience with at least a 25% stake in the SPV. And if the builder has a 25% stake in the project, not only will they be paid the standard profit they priced into agreeing to construct the job but also a 25% share in the business.

Before agreeing to any of this though, you need to make sure that the builder complies with the FCA PS13/3 policy statement, as previously discussed in chapter 8, as you are offering them an equity or profit share.

You could also structure it that if you build eight houses, the builder retains ownership of two as their 25% stake. You may even want to consider doing a 50/50, if you are looking to do this for a while. There are plenty of ways to structure such a deal.

Activity creates opportunity. – Andi Cooke

Secret Tip #15: Every obstruction has a solution. If you have no track record that's fine, it can be borrowed. You can joint venture. Some lenders will be happy for a very experienced power team to drive the project. Money should not stop you developing. Time should not get in the way. Go back to the obstacles section of the book in chapter 6 to recap this.

Chapter 14 Sharing Our Expertise

During the development of St James, the property investment community we met with regularly were keen to find out how we had built a development using none of our own money, as the way we raised the finance for the development, over £750,000 of private investments and through crowdfunding, was innovative at the time. We were more than happy to help.

In the traditional business model, competition is rife. Companies don't want to reveal what they are doing and how they are doing it because they fear their competitors will copy them and, worse, beat them to the market or steal their potential customers.

Property investing, however, is different. Most of us are very willing to share what we do, how we do it, how much we made, and even tips on how to do what we do more easily.

There are millions of properties out there and no one developer can purchase and develop all of them. Not only are there enough to go round but when other developers complete quality projects where we are developing, it strengthens the market. Win-win.

So, sharing our business model was something we were more than happy to do. We don't consider ourselves any different to other people. Anyone can get into property developments, just like we did. And it is down to them whether they choose to pursue it.

Andi and I were open, we were honest, and we shared the ups and downs of our journey. We invited people to come see our St James site, talked them through the funding process, and introduced them to Funding Circle, our crowdfunding platform. Some big names in property, we said, have done some amazing things by using Funding Circle after we introduced them to it, as it was still a rarity in the property development finance world back then. They pre-funded the development, quite different to most others lenders who typically lend retrospectively, that is, only after the developer has invested (or raised) a considerable amount up front.

Public speaking was new to us, although I did have a sales background so I wasn't too nervous, and so we agreed to give a few 20-minute talks at property network meetings to explain how Funding Circle had helped us. Those 20 minutes soon stretched to an hour, what with all the questions we were fielding. That talk soon changed to one about how we had done the deals using none of our own money, as we tried to help as many people as possible. After all, we had needed the help when we first started.

Andi and I both spoke initially, until we decided that I would handle that part of the presentation while he handled the onsite tours. This way we could split our time and help more people get started. We didn't really think of it as training per se because we weren't focused on the fact that what we had been doing was so different from what was taught in seminars and such.

Even more people approached us after the St James development won us the Deal of the Year in December 2014 and we spent considerable time over the next four months showing individuals around our site. That's when I suggested to Andi that it would be far more efficient to organise a formal class rather than speak to people individually. That was when White Box Property Solutions shifted its focus to provide formal training sessions.

Our first course took place in July 2015, just a year and a half after we had begun collaborating on our first development. We had 18 people sign up for what was then a two-day course, all people whom we knew who had watched us from the start.

Since it was our first training course, we priced it very low, offered a two-for-the-price-of-one enrolment, and arranged for a representative of Funding Circle to make a short presentation as a bonus.

The feedback was tremendously positive, and we discovered that we really enjoyed showing people how to do what we were doing. They say the fear of public speaking is shared by almost everyone, and I'd certainly never envisioned myself doing it, never mind enjoying it, but as it turned out, I love it. I love helping others. It's the reason why I chose to write this book.

We organised another session in November 2015, and a third in January 2016, this time to a group of 30, ranging from complete beginners to some very experienced property investors who bought individual properties for single buy-to-lets and were hoping to expand. There were also three architects who wanted to design their own developments rather than do it for somebody else.

The group also included a husband and wife duo, Simon and Mel, who had a building company and had been building other people's houses for 35 years but had been hit hard by the recession. They wanted to get into property developments for themselves, but were now gun-shy, despite having so much building experience. Simon and Mel have since done a small, no-money-down development, but as Mel shares here, it opened up a new world for them.

Mel's story

In January 1984, I stood outside a ramshackle old cob cottage. The lad who'd been the technician at the studio pottery, before I succeeded as an apprentice, popped his head out of the doorway and led me to the back of the garden where an old greenhouse stood.

'I'll take it,' I said. 'How much is it?'

'It's free to a good home', he replied. 'I'll drop it by tomorrow.' Three months later, we were engaged. Five months later, we were married. He was 23 and I was 21. The ramshackle old cob cottage, two up, two down, was now home.

It needed major work.

Simon had already removed a dilapidated shed at the back and a digger was booked in for the footings for the new extension. Our married life began with building.

For three years we spent every evening and every weekend creating our beautiful cottage home, doubling it in size to create a quintessential cottage garden in its third of an acre, constructing a double garage and wood store and renovating an old barn that was to be my first pottery studio workshop.

Three years and two children later, with our lovely home now complete, Simon, now a site carpenter for large building companies, was growing frustrated. Having learned to work on price and produce high quality work efficiently was something that would serve us well in the future, but he despaired at the overall disorganisation and incompetency of the sites he was assigned. At age 29, convinced he could do better on his own, he started his own business working for private clients on refurbishments, renovations, and bespoke new builds.

During this period, we saw a small, unloved terraced house for sale and thought it might be a good investment to renovate, which we did, and rented it out to our brother-in-law's sister. That was our first rental property.

Alongside working for private clients, Simon purchased a site with planning for a large bungalow and changed the planning to three houses. We sold two and kept one for ourselves, which became rental number two.

Next, we found ourselves a listed barn to convert, the old Apple barn. It was a beautiful building with an acre of ground and an ancient, fruitful apple tree. We doubled the size of the barn, very carefully and thoughtfully designing the extension ourselves to perfectly blend with the original barn. To match the old painted bricks, we bought new concrete bricks and tumbled twenty thousand of them in the cement mixer to mimic the wear and tear of the original brickwork and used them to build the outer skin. When painted, you could not tell the difference. We were delighted. With just a bit of thought and care, we realised, it was possible to work harmoniously with an old building.

Inside, we managed to keep all the original roof structure and boarded it out with reclaimed timber boarding and replaced the upstairs floors with reclaimed floorboards. The staircases were made in our joinery workshop, again from reclaimed wood.

We needed a chunky design for the staircase and so we mocked up a life-size set of stairs out of cardboard and paper, in situ, to be sure we got the proportions just right. (These days we sketch it and work with architects, but it was great experience to do it all ourselves, as it enabled us to intimately understand design and how to work with the framework and structure of an old building, taking into consideration scale and proportion.)

Meanwhile, we were outgrowing our darling little cottage now that the children were older, and I wanted more garden space. In addition, the farm next door operated 24/7 and the relentless noise had become unpleasant. It was whilst doing this first barn project, we purchased another, some 15 minutes away, what had been an old riding school, many years before. It was already huge, so it needed no extension, and the roof had already been done. We converted an additional barn onsite into a workshop and store and exchanged an option on five acres of land up the lane for one adjacent acre behind ours, which greatly increased its value. We lived in this beautiful five-bedroom, five-en-suite former riding academy for nine months, before moving on again, still hunting for that perfect place to call home and settle for the next fifty years.

In between times, we purchased a lovely old threshing barn with a beautiful roundhouse set overlooking the loveliest of Devon's valleys. A fantastic spot, it was sold before we built it. That turned out to have been a mistake, as the market rose dramatically over that eight-month period and we lost out hugely.

Never mind, you live and learn. The old farmhouse opposite, with its asbestos roof and water pouring in, failed to sell at the height of the market. We contacted an agent friend who located the owner and eventually purchased it, managing to acquire an acre of land behind the house as well. We then split the farmhouse in two, building an extension onto each side, and split the additional acre, assigning a half acre to each property. One we sold, and one we rented out as a holiday let, which was nominated for a Gold Award for excellence. That marked the start of ten years of high-end holiday letting.

Next, we purchased an old farmhouse in need of attention, which the previous owner had asserted, 'All it needs is a lick of paint'. We gutted the place completely, built on an extension, and ended up with a fabulous five-bedroom five-en-suite home, with a one-bedroom annexe attached, a big double garage, and an acre of land just five minutes from the sea. That was our next holiday cottage, which at one point would be booked for 42 weeks straight. It would also be highly acclaimed and we used it as the letting company's flagship property.

After that came a house bought at auction, a miserable 1960s bungalow surrounded by massive fir trees. Its gold lay in the fact that it was within walking distance of the estuary beach, and lay adjacent to the Royal North Devon Golf Club and the Northam Burrows, an area of special scientific interest and a country park. We converted this into another five-bedroom, five-en-suite house, which proved a fantastic challenge to incorporate interest and good design into a bungalow, but it proved well worth the effort. It was highly praised by everyone who saw it and rented out as a hugely successful holiday let.

Then we found it – the place we wanted to make our home. It was an ugly mishmash of a farmhouse that had obviously missed out on anyone with an understanding about buildings.

That didn't matter. We knew we could turn it into whatever we liked. The magic? Its position, set in the centre of a 42-acre piece of land, plenty of space for us to expand into over the next fifty years – space to create lakes, to plant woodland, and to create a beautiful natural environment filled with myriad wild species of plant and animal. A wildlife sanctuary to teach and inspire. Space to develop our gardens, to have our workshops, to build walled gardens, to create an arboretum, and to teach the heritage skills we so love. It was heady to contemplate.

Such dreams.

Six years later, in 2008, our world came crashing down.

In the middle of a big conversion project of a chapel and schoolhouse, the banks demanded their money back, complete with debt collectors who hounded us three times a day. We realised we were going to lose everything, including our precious home and all we had worked for.

One morning we looked at each other and said no. We would

fight this.

And we did. We clawed our way back, managing by the skin of our teeth to hold on to our home and our properties. Slowly, but surely, we built a new business working for private clients once again. With our understanding of and respect for old buildings, we were never short of work, and we gradually dug ourselves out of the deep, deep hole we'd been thrust into.

We trained in business. We trained in marketing. And then we trained in property.

Property? Why, when we already had so much experience?

We wanted to get back into developments and do it right this time, but our confidence had been shattered, having been hit so hard by the recession. We trained through Progressive Property in Peterborough, learning the many strategies available.

It was at one of these meetings where we had a roundtable talk with two guys about their recent development. Andi Cooke, one of the partners, was a former builder, so we could relate to him. What these guys, Andi and Lloyd, had achieved in such a short time was amazing. There was something about them, something we could connect with, and what they said rang true.

We met them on several occasions after that, and at one point Lloyd mentioned they were going to start up some training, not to teach people how to build but how they had managed to build a property investing business so quickly, with little or no personal capital. We were interested but not swayed until Andi said he could help Simon transition again from builder to developer. We bought their course, and as one of the first few, we received a complimentary mastermind day.

This was at the start of 2016, and I remember clearly how both of us were blown away by their course. They were so open about how they got started and what it takes to do it. I liked their honest approach. We realised this was a direction we had to follow in order to regain the confidence to get back into developments.

At the time, we were in the middle of purchasing a lovely old listed house in Bideford that we have since converted into an HMO, yet it wasn't what we really wanted to do. Andi and Lloyd's emphasis was on build-to-rent, a strategy that appealed to us, although we realised that, to begin with, we would need to flip to take the great weight of the mortgage off our backs and protect our precious home.

We attended the mastermind session and came away convinced we could learn so much from these guys and the contacts they were creating. This was despite the fact that we had more building experience than both of them put together! The thing was, so much had changed in the ten years we'd been out of the development market, and we'd lost all confidence. We needed to learn how to do things differently. And so it started, the wonderful, phoenix-like rising from the ashes.

Never mind the six-hour drive to Northampton each month – that was irrelevant. What was invaluable was the encouragement, the knowledge, the information, and the networking. This compounded, and by the end of the first year we had gained back part of our confidence and bought our first development project in eleven years, two beautiful stone barns. It's like riding a bike, we discovered. You never forget, so it's easy to get back into the swing of things. Except that now it is different. We had to step back, grow our team again, and allow others to do most of the work.

These days, our son works in the business with us, someone who understands the way we do things. He's a huge asset who manages the site. Any problems we hit, we know we can get over because of the access we now have to knowledge and expertise in all parts of the development world. Andi and Lloyd have been central in helping us return to developments. The confidence they have given us to just get on with it again cannot be measured. We are now in the second half of our second year with them. As I write this, the two stone barns are about ten to twelve weeks from completion and we're in the process of acquiring our next project of three barns.

As well as this, we are in talks with the owners of a possible 27-house conversion site, almost a ready-made village as Lloyd and Andi teasingly describe it. And then there's another site of five architect-designed houses and several other exciting projects in the pipeline.

Without Lloyd and Andi's help, we would have struggled to change our thinking, let alone consider all these other projects at the same time. I can truly say that working with Lloyd and Andi has been a life-changing experience. And each month, when we meet at a mastermind session, we return home with even more valuable nuggets which still surprises and delights us. The value they continue to provide is huge.

As a direct result, our business has changed. Not only have we once again built up a team of great craftsman and professionals, we now raise finance through commercial funders as well as work with private lenders and investors. This is an important part for us, being able to share a slice of the profit pie with friends, family, and our wider circle.

Going forward, with a renewed confidence and realisation of our capabilities, we plan to carry on with our barn conversions as well as work on larger development projects.

We have also been asked to joint venture in additional development projects in our beautiful area, and we still dream of creating that ancient woodland and wildlife sanctuary where we can share our love of heritage crafts and so much more – far larger, wider-reaching dreams which will help many of our young and underprivileged.

Andi and Lloyd have been instrumental in helping us win back our confidence to move ahead. With their knowledge, experience, and phenomenal driving force in their own business, and their willingness to generously share all their contacts, procedures, and strategies with us, it makes for a very powerful and invaluable team.

Hugely exciting times ahead!

You may, upon reading this, think, yeah but Mel and Simon already had tonnes of experience so getting into developments was easier for them. Yes, they did have considerable experience, but they also came within a thread of losing everything, including their home, when the recession hit. It frightened them, scarring them to the point where their fear was arguably a far bigger hurdle than someone with no experience starting fresh. Andi and I are enormously proud of having shown them how to set aside those fears and return to their real love, doing developments, and taking it far beyond what they'd originally envisioned. That 27-house conversion site Mel mentions is underway is a village. It is a fantastic development project and one that I am delighted to help with.

January is always a popular month for people to make changes, to start the year differently. New Year's resolutions kick in: New Year, New Me. Matt is another example of someone who, since taking our January 2017 course, has achieved a great deal from taking action, shifting to a strategy of rent-to-rent HMOs and

SAs, serviced accommodation.

Matt's story

I have always wanted to get into property development. University days were spent watching Homes Under the Hammer and Grand Designs, thinking, 'I can't wait to build my own house' but that I probably couldn't afford to start developing property until I was at least forty years old.

I saw Andi and Lloyd present at a property event and was impressed with how much they had achieved in such a short period of time, which motivated me to pull my finger out and get on with it. Before the course I had several rent-to-rent HMOs and SAs, along with my single-lets portfolio.

After taking their January course, my company, Homes Cornwall, formed an SPV with local investors and purchased a site on which we're developing three two-bed houses. One is a major renovation which didn't require planning and is now complete. The other two have been granted planning and we are just signing off the building regulations drawings.

I chose to join their monthly mastermind group, which has been hugely beneficial to my business, providing access to planners, brokers, project managers, and other property professionals, the benefits of which have been immediate.

For our current project, instead of getting a main contractor to do the build, I chose to manage the project myself. Originally, the site was envisioned for two houses, but after speaking with the mastermind group, we increased it to three, and had no problems getting it through planning. The support from the community and mentors of the mastermind group has given me the knowledge, systems, and confidence to think on a bigger scale. My understanding of construction has increased significantly and it also means that we have saved 15–20% in costs, which is directly evident in the bottom-line profit.

I particularly value the mastermind group because a lot of us start out on our own, or as a partnership, and unlike other businesses, we aren't directly surrounded by like-minded individuals who understand property and developing. Being part of the mastermind group gives us support and motivation, both of which are huge contributors to our success.

The business is going from strength, taking on an office unit and growing the team by another two part-time staff, and advertising for an acquisitions manager to join us. We currently have two offers in with agents and another three sites being appraised, our intention being to establish a pipeline of two to three projects on the go at any given time. The plan is to grow the company to a small, highly efficient team, designed to give me sufficient time and freedom to focus on other projects and spend time with my family.

The mastermind sessions that we run provide help and further guidance for those who take our courses. Property developments are an in-depth strategy, one that takes time, patience, and work. Because the market changes, the mastermind sessions are monthly, with ongoing support not just from Andi and me but also from our power team members, our project manager, planning consultant, and our commercial finance broker. The mastermind support program will continue to grow, and we will continue to offer support, for as long as possible. We are not gurus in property and never claim to be. We are supporters and property developers.

People who take action get results. You've got to be in it to win it, as they say. If you don't buy a lottery ticket, how can you ever expect to win the lottery? Or as renowned Canadian ice hockey player Wayne Gretzky famously said, 'You miss one hundred per cent of the shots you don't take'.

Paul is proof of this. Paul did the course very recently and we were delighted to learn that within weeks he had sourced a deal. The offer was accepted and he started the process. Several weeks after that, he had another deal accepted.

Paul's story

Like most adults, my priorities totally changed when my daughter was born in 2010. I can track my journey into build-to-rent back to that very moment. By then I'd already been running my own business for five years.

I had started my adult life as a newspaper reporter before moving on to become a newsreader, radio presenter, and programme controller across a load of radio stations in the Midlands. It was great fun. But after 13 years spent working for someone else, I was feeling the triple pain of a) no spare cash, b) no spare time, and c) no control over what I did, or when. Every night I arrived home, tired and grumpy, and spent most of the evening whinging about the day I'd had.

Sundays were the worst. The feeling of dread started to creep in around lunchtime when I realised that the treadmill of pointless work was about to restart. By bedtime on Sunday night I was miserable again.

I've since learned that you have to listen very closely to your deepest, innermost feelings. They are translations of your mind's desires. They inform you what you really want in life. And if you don't act on them, you run the risk of waking up aged 70, regretting what you've done (or haven't done) with your life.

At the end, only a few people actually regret the things they've done. But the majority do express regret over the things they wanted to do but didn't.

See, I REALLY wanted to start my own business. I wanted to wrest control over my time. I wasn't afraid of hard work, but I wanted to personally benefit from it, rather than help a large media group add a few pennies to its share price.

I was reading all the right books on starting a business. I had a good enough plan. I'd got our personal finances into good shape.

Yet I didn't do it.

Why?

Simple.

Fear. Or as I now know it, FEAR: Fictional Events Appearing Real.

The fear of the unknown. The what-if's. The worry about what could happen if I started my business and failed.

Fear, and its partner, Worry, are two of the worst criminals I have ever met. They're very sneaky. They start small, establish a foothold, then slowly get bigger and bigger inside our hearts, until they dominate, and suffocate our decision-making abilities.

We make most decisions with our heart. We might think we're making decisions logically using our brains but, nope – the heart makes the decisions based on our emotions. The brain just rubber stamps them.

So, if Fear and Worry become our dominant emotions, they drive the decisions we make, ones that don't allow us to move forward. Fear and Worry hold us back.

Luckily, I found a magic bullet with which to shoot Fear and Worry. Sometimes it kills them dead. The rest of the time it wounds them badly enough that I can make the right decision regardless of their presence.

That magic bullet? It's ACTION.

ACTION is my best friend. I keep it loaded in my gun, and make sure to fire off several ACTION bullets every day. No matter how badly something is going, ACTION ultimately saves me.

This has proven to be the case in my build-to-rent strategy, as well as with my business career. In fact, ACTION encouraged me to skive off work one day to attend a seminar on starting your own business. I nearly didn't do it because Worry told me I might get caught and fired. Even at the door of the hotel where the event was, I nearly turned away and went in to work instead.

But instead I fired a bullet at it – and oh, what a magical event that was. I can remember how I felt talking to people just like me and realising it was utterly possible to create the life I really wanted to live. The effect of that day has lived with me ever since, discovering that I didn't have to do anything new and scary on my own, that there are always people to help me.

When you surround yourself with the right people, you think the right way. The late entrepreneur Jim Rohn notably said that we comprise the average of the five people we spend the most time with.

I've worked very hard over the years to remove the negative people from my life. There's no room for doubters and haters when you're on a mission to create the life you truly deserve. The night of that seminar I went home bursting with excitement and energy for the first time in years. And after a long conversation with my wife, Helen, the world's most wonderful and supportive person, we agreed I would quit my job the next day. And I did. Just like that, I gave my three months' notice and handed back my £60,000 package – my top-of-the-range Saab 9-3, big pension, and company BlackBerry – or the DoomBringer, as I used to call it, as it only ever delivered depressing news to me.

Twelve months later I'd replaced my salary by running a marketing business from my spare room, and was looking for office premises and to hire my first employee.

The business did alright over the next few years. I kept firing ACTION bullets and it grew well. But I didn't realise I was following the wrong strategy. That's because I'd become a busy fool. I was spending too much time working IN my business, and very little time working ON it. The whole business was overly reliant upon me. Although I had two employees by now, nothing really happened unless I made it happen. And that created a massive burden on me.

I had begun to feel trapped, that I'd created a prison of my own design and had locked myself inside. Then came the wakeup call. My daughter Tilda, who was due in October, arrived without warning in mid July, fifteen weeks premature, after just an hour's labour. The Special Care Baby Unit doctors warned us she might not survive the night. Thankfully, she did.

For the three months after Tilda's birth, I focused on my family. I kept in contact with the business, but I wasn't there, mentally or physically. The day I eventually did return to work, after being absent for three months, I found myself dreading it. Would there even be a viable business to return to? Or would it have taken a massive step backwards?

In reality, the opposite was true. My two staff had stepped up to the mark and essentially replaced me. They were keeping the marketing going, selling to clients, and delivering. More astonishing was the fact that the business was running more efficiently than when I had spent 12 hours every day running it myself.

I felt a little hurt at first, I confess. For most business owners, our identity is tied up with our business. But it wore off quickly and I realised how exciting this was. Because now I had space, space to stand back and work ON the business, rather than IN it.

I stopped going into the office so much, and started working from McDonald's, Costa, and Starbucks – anywhere I could get power and Wi-Fi became my office.

I took more time off. I went on more holidays, including a two-week cruise with zero internet or phone contact – sheer bliss. In 2012, we moved to a new home in Milton Keynes, an hour from the office. I started only going in on Thursday mornings.

Suddenly, I had a business that was there for me, rather than the other way around. And the growth continued at an impressive rate every year. From 2010 to 2011 the business grew its turnover by 47%. The year after, it grew by 67%. We reached seven-figure turnover and six-figure net profit. And on the 24th March 2016, I sold the business to a fast-growing digital marketing agency for an undisclosed sum.

What was my secret? What did I actually do to grow the business to the point it could be sold as a profitable, ongoing concern?

Back in 2010, the year my daughter was born, I had sought out a mentor, someone who had already completed the journey I was on, to advise me.

My business mentor – who is now one of my best friends – helped me to step back and see the bigger picture. He didn't tell me what to do. Instead, he helped me to understand the problems I was facing and guided me to make the right decisions – and to understand why they were the right decisions, so I was actually learning whilst firing off ACTION bullets.

I've since secured a mentor for every new venture I've undertaken. When you are accountable to a mentor, you take bigger and more focused ACTION, and ultimately achieve better results with fewer mistakes.

So, there I was, in spring, 2016, with a little money on my hands and loads of time. I did what every flush former business owner apparently does: the month of driving hours just to have lunch with an old friend; the month of boredom drinking; the month where you test drive Aston Martins just because you can...

After six months, my wife advised me to go back to work. I pondered what that might be. I wanted something that provided me both solid cash flow and free time. I had grown to love the quality time I now had to spend with my wife and daughter. But I needed cash to do that, and the one downside of selling your business is removing your income stream.

I started to buy and sell businesses for fun, and income. But I was also starting to think seriously about my asset base and what would leave for my daughter, as a friend had recently died from cancer and it reminded me I wasn't going to last forever.

I'd also dreamt of creating three-generational wealth. What if I could leave behind an asset base to benefit my daughter, her children, and her children's children? What if, in a hundred years' time, a distant relative of mine raised a glass of Prosecco to my memory, because I had put them through the world's best cyber college or something? What a cool legacy!

Property seemed to be the way forward. I had a small number of single lets – nothing to write home about – but I could see that property would give me another income stream and create an asset base.

I decided I would buy a single let every six months, get it refurbished, and recycle my cash into the next one.

I didn't realise that my property strategy was years out of date until I went to a property networking meeting and heard Lloyd Girardi speak.

Just like the business seminar I'd attended all those years before, it was one of those moments I'll never forget. A shiver ran down my spine as he explained build-to-rent.

Screw growing by just two units a year! Screw paying George Osborne's extra stamp duty. All those legal fees. And his Section 24 tenant tax. Here was a smart and proven strategy that would allow me to grow my portfolio by 10 units or more EVERY YEAR. And cost me considerably less money than buying single lets. That's the definition of a no-brainer.

I signed up for the introductory Discovery Day, and from there went on to do the three-day Property Developers' Secrets course. In it, Lloyd and Andi laid out everything I needed to do, step by step, to become a build-to-rent property developer. They had been there and done it. They'd made loads of mistakes, ones that I could learn from.

The Sunday night after the course I couldn't sleep. It was 11 p.m. and I was bursting with excitement. I was actually annoyed that I had to sleep. The adrenalin was flowing, and I couldn't wait to get up and start the process. In my mind, I ran over the key lessons I had learned from my business journey, and how applicable they were as I started this new phase of my life.

Trust your gut. My emotions were telling me this was the correct *path forward, and I was desperate to follow them. I didn't need to overthink this decision. I trusted my gut feeling.*

Fear and Worry are easily killed by ACTION. As excited as I was, I was also utterly terrified. I'm as bad as Lloyd at DIY. I have no construction abilities whatsoever. I briefly allowed Worry to run a series of disastrous scenarios in my mind about all the things that could go wrong. And then I loaded my mental gun with a round of ACTION bullets. Whatever problems I faced, I could use ACTION to overcome them.

Surround yourself with the right people. I'd committed to joining a White Box mentoring group because if I wanted to be a build-to-rent property developer, then I needed to be associated with other build-to-rent property developers. Lying there in bed, I realised I didn't know what I didn't know. But I knew the right supportive environment would help me learn quickly.

Find the right mentor. A mentor would be key to this new journey. Lloyd and Andi were on a path I wanted to follow. After spending three days with them, I trusted them. I could see they would help me get to where I wanted to be much faster than if I tried to do it alone.

I leapt out of bed at 5am the next morning. I've always been an early riser, as I find it a great time to get things done. I spent the next twelve hours in my office, taking massive action.

It was almost too easy. The three-day course is built around a comprehensive workbook that contains all of the learning and your own notes. I knew the first White Box step was to Find it – so I opened the workbook at the appropriate page and just did what I had been taught.

I looked at sites on Google Maps, bought title deeds, printed out letters, and posted them. I searched online for architects and rang to introduce myself. I contacted commercial agents and scoured commercial sites on Rightmove.

The next day I did the same. And again on the third day. I started putting in formal offers left, right, and centre. They were much lower than the inflated asking prices, but I was building momentum and gaining valuable experience in how to deal with agents and sellers.

The way Lloyd and Andi taught me to offer gave me huge credibility with sellers, despite the fact that I was still in 'Fake it till you make it' mode. And I'm sure some of those formal offers will bounce back to me in the future as deals fall through and agents dig out old correspondence.

I had meeting after meeting after meeting. I screwed some up, which taught me some valuable lessons. Others went very well. I ramped up my property networking in Milton Keynes to spread the word on what I was looking for. I set up a personal website and improved my Facebook and LinkedIn profiles.

At the same time, with an eye on White Box's second step of Fund it, I started working my network to find my first investors. Lloyd had advised me that I needed to do these two find and fund steps simultaneously, so I could act with speed when I did find a site.

Looking back, it was an insane couple of weeks. And it felt great, because I was firing off ACTION bullets all day, every day. I absolutely trusted one hundred per cent that this would work, because I was doing exactly what Lloyd and Andi had done. I was expecting to get the same results. And I did.

A few weeks after starting, I got a call out of the blue from a residential estate agent I had introduced myself to. It just so happened he had a piece of land with lapsed planning permission for four three-bedroom semi-detached houses. Would I be interested?

Two hours later I had completed my initial desktop appraisal, created a formal offer pack, and submitted it to the agent. I'd also set up a meeting with him the next morning to run through the offer and discuss any concerns his seller might have. (My secret agenda for that meeting was to build my credibility – if an agent believes in you, they will promote your offer to their seller in a much more convincing way.)

There was another moment I'll never forget, when the agent rang.

'Despite your offer being £18,000 below the asking price, my vendors will accept it on the condition that it's a cash deal and you can complete quickly.'

Boom!

The ACTION bullets had just hit their target. And my career as a property developer had truly started.

The second site followed just a week or so later. This was a riskier site, with only a 50/50 chance of getting planning permission for a couple of detached bungalows according to White Box's planning consultant. So instead of buying the site, I signed a long-option agreement, giving me time to gain planning permission for the site before I had to buy it.

Only two months had elapsed since I had completed the Property Developers' Secrets course and I had managed to secure my first two sites, with a combined GDV of £1.5 million, and a combined forecasted profit of £372,000. Not bad. Two small deals to get me started. At time of writing, the first site is about to exchange and complete. (I confess I ignored Lloyd's advice about financing and which solicitor to use, which slowed the deal down and required urgent fixes. Doh! Lesson learnt.)

Once that site is secured, I will ramp up my site-finding activity again to continue building my deals pipeline. Lloyd suggests a little activity every day, which seems a sensible way to have it constantly simmering in the background.

My property goal now is to build and keep 10 to 20 units a year for a few years and see where that takes me. As my confidence and competence grow, I might get hungry for bigger deals. I'll keep listening to and following my gut as I go along. There's still plenty I don't know, and loads of mistakes I will make, but I have the right support structure and mentors to help me through whatever challenges lie ahead.

I'm very grateful to Lloyd and Andi for lighting the path and so generously sharing their knowledge and experience.

You miss 100% of the shots you don't take. – Wayne Gretzky

Secret Tip #16: When will you start? What has been holding you back? Maybe it is a lack of knowledge or money. Whatever has been stopping you in the past can, if you permit it, stop your future. Please take time to view our website and see what we can offer. From Discovery Days to Retreats, whatever your ability, we can help. You help yourself first by allowing yourself to learn and start taking action.

Chapter 15 Activity Creates Opportunity

There's no such thing as luck. Andi and I both believe this. People make their own luck – or, more likely, they make their own opportunity. Movie mogul Sam Goldwyn was quoted as saying, 'The harder I work, the luckier I get'. 'Luck' is the positive outcome of activity. The more effort you put in, the more opportunities are presented to you. It isn't luck. It's work. As Andi is fond of saying, activity is what creates opportunity.

Some people have said that we were 'fortunate' to get into developments. It wasn't fortunate that my dad and grandad passed away when they did; it was life. Unfortunately, life kicks you in the bollocks sometimes, but it's how you respond that reveals who you really are. Adversity can either knock you on your arse or make you stronger – it's your choice.

Before I started my own business, I never paid much attention to frequently quoted sayings, beyond acknowledging they were truisms people would parrot in support of their viewpoints. They were just words. But these days, having gotten into developments, having developed our business, more of these observations have begun to resonate with me. That's why I've sprinkled several of my favourite ones throughout this book, the ones that mean the most to me, those which carry the most significance in terms of all I've learned on this journey.

These include two from Zig Ziglar:

You don't have to be great to start, but you have to start to be great,

and

F-E-A-R has two meanings: Forget Everything And Run, or Face

Everything And Rise. The choice is yours.

Another, this one by ice-hockey legend Wayne Gretzky:

You miss one hundred per cent of the shots you don't take.

And from Richard Branson:

I have always believed that there is no point in having regrets as you learn far more from mistakes than successes. Embrace a mistake and learn from it; don't regret them.

And the last, often attributed to Albert Einstein although no one is really sure if he ever said it, is worth repeating:

Insanity is doing the same thing over and over and expecting a different result.

Don't wait until you're great – being great at something takes practice. It means you have to do it over and over so that you can become great at it. Start now and get perfect later. Otherwise you'll never take that first step, and you'll regret never starting.

Don't miss your shot because you hesitated and never took it.

Do you know the wealthiest place in the world? It's the graveyard. How many unfulfilled intentions lie buried there? How many untold stories, unwritten books, potential inventions, and new businesses never started remain under the surface?

If you want change, make it. Do something different. Don't let fear hold you back. If our fears didn't hold us back so often, there wouldn't be so many books on the subject. Susan Jeffers wrote Feel the Fear and Do It Anyway, on how we can turn our fear into confidence.

Don't be afraid of making mistakes, but do be sensible. Learn from your mistakes but don't jump into the deep end when you haven't first learned to tread water. Start small. That might be a small site to start with, less than 10 houses. Keep it simple and learn the ropes.

Once you start, and stick with it, more opportunities will come your way. Andi and I receive development opportunities regularly because people know that's what we do, and because we created the opportunity for people to send us deals. We created opportunity by taking action. Start living the life you have always dreamt of instead of just dreaming about it. I dreamt of starting a business years before I did, but I didn't do anything back then to make it a reality. Now that I have made it a reality, I only wish I had started earlier.

Actions speak louder than words. Take action.

Create your vision board or dream board and place it somewhere visible, somewhere you can look at it every day. (See Secret Tip #8, at the end of chapter 6.) Subconsciously, you will mentally return to what's on your vision board and the law of attraction will guide you to achieve your vision. Take a moment now and picture your dreams. Soak them in and imagine how good it feels to achieve something you have long desired.

What's an OSM?

OSM is a term that was coined by one of our students, Mitul, who emailed it to us following a mentoring session. It is a situation that everyone, and certainly most new property developers, experience at some point, even if most are not familiar with the term OSM.

An OSM is an 'Oh, shit!' moment.

You know the moment. The moment you realise that what you

are doing is different, that you've just jumped into the deep end and found yourself in unfamiliar waters. The moment that you realise that this is big, this needs to be considered carefully, as it will potentially change your life. The moment when you realise that you are an actual property developer. You are doing it. It's that moment that you are in the captain's chair, piloting your future to its destination, and you are in control.

The OSM realisation comes at different times for different people, depending on their history, but you will experience it, I promise you that.

You might experience your first OSM when your first offer is accepted on a plot of land. It might happen when you first appraise a site, crunch the numbers, and you feel a frisson of excitement when you discover it works.

It may come in the middle of the night. (no, not that OSM!) You may experience it when you stand onsite and watch your development commence.

OSMs are great, but they can also feel daunting. They make you sit back, look at what you have achieved to date, and realise that you might need help going forward as things expand –mentors, networking events, business partners, even a life partner.

Whatever help you need going forward, don't be afraid to ask. Seek advice. Most people will be flattered to be asked, and more than you might realise are generous in giving assistance.

This might be a new venture for you. But it could be a venture that will reward you handsomely. Embrace the moment and ride the wave.

Thanks to Mitul for putting such an apt name to the feeling.

If you experience an OSM using the procedures outlined in this book, tweet me at @whiteboxps, or join our Facebook community on the group Property Developers Secrets, and use the hashtag #OSM.

Our own OSMs

In 2014, when we started, we went through many OSMs, not all of which we consciously recognised as such at the time. But we had them, just as you will have them. But unlike you, what we didn't have was a book, a course, or a mentor guiding us through a development. We learnt the hard way.

I want you to learn from us. Why? Because even though we are not perfect, we're honest. Every new day presents the possibility of a new learning experience and we continue to improve. We are growing our company every day.

We now have a portfolio manager looking after all of our properties. We have a project manager, whose experience includes having worked for one of the UK's largest house builders, typically managing a site of 80–100 houses a year, who now oversees all of our projects. We have a financial director. We have an accounts team, which includes our accountants and tax specialists who, to be fair, keep us in check. We have a contracts team and sub-contractors who we call upon when we need them. We have a community of likeminded developers who are on the same journey as we are. We have mentors whom we can call upon when we need guidance or advice, and we have our wives who support us whilst we continue to build our business, knowing that the business will look after our families.

Here are some of the OSMs we experienced after starting out.

Oh, shit...

- We've just bought a plot of land at auction for £157,000!

- We have to find £157,000 in just 28 days!

- We have no money!

- We only have two weeks left to complete on the plot of land!

- We're putting in our very first planning application on a plot of land that we now own!

- That cost more than we thought!

- We need to find a development finance lender to fund £600,000!

- Look at the forms we have to fill out to secure a development lender!

- This is it – the first day of our build stage!

- The copper pipes that were just delivered onsite yesterday have been stolen!

- It's time to talk to letting agents about advertising our properties!

- We need to apply for our first commercial finance re-mortgage!

- We're limited in the number of lenders available to us because we didn't do our due diligence first and speak to the broker at the start of the development!

- We're actually filling out the paperwork for a commercial finance lender!

- Our lender doesn't accept a Professional Consultant's Certificate and we don't have a new-build warranty in place!

- We're gonna be able to rent out our new properties for more than we expected!

- Our GDV is higher than we expected!

- British Telecom is wait-listing us when we need phone lines installed in our units, leaving our new tenants without internet! (Double-OSM!)

- The refinance stage is gonna take HOW long?

- We just received a mortgage offer for £890,000 on our first completed development!

- All of a sudden our equity has leapt up to £370,000!

- We've now got a gross monthly cash flow of nearly £6,500, of which £3,200 a month is net to us, and we've got eight properties in our portfolio!

- Built-to-rent actually works!

- *Let's do it again!*

Believe me, those were some serious OSMs for us. Some were very real challenges, but we worked through them together, found the answers we needed, and carried on developing. We didn't let the challenges stop us.

The moment you stop – the moment you let fear paralyse you – is the moment you fail.

Some of our success was timing, some of it circumstance. Having Andi with his renovation experience as a business partner from the start helped us to excel at what we were doing. I certainly wouldn't have started developing if it hadn't been for Andi phoning me that 27th December 2013. I was ready to change my life and take on a challenge. I was ready to finally start my dream of owning my own business.

Andi would likely still be doing one site at a time instead of several if he hadn't considered partnering.

Our training business would never have materialised if I hadn't forced Andi out of his comfort zone and into public speaking. It wasn't comfortable at first for either of us, but I knew it would be a great way to share our story with others who were thinking about property developments as a way to change and improve their lives.

Andi and I share the same vision, drive, and determination, the same aspiration to continue to succeed, and our strengths and what we bring to the table complement each other. I consider myself the bigger thinker in terms of growing the company and pushing ourselves to the next level – maybe too optimistically sometimes.

Having Andi to bounce off ideas and work on the business together has been nothing less than fantastic. We are at a point now where I can focus on our training business, White Box Property Solutions, and help others get into developments whilst Andi focuses on overseeing our development sites.

We work well together and we love helping people. We love to give back and share.

We do it differently to most people. We maintain an honest and professional business whilst making it fun!

We do it the White Box way.

Let us know if you've enjoyed the book. In fact, send us a photo of you reading it, no matter where you are, at @whiteboxps #whiteboxway. We'd love to hear from you!

Helpful Professional Contacts

<u>Finance</u>

Broker   Pilot Fish

                                 2 Manning Road

                                 Bourne, Peterborough PE10 9HW

                                 01778 309 777

                                 http://www.pilotfishpartnership.co.uk

Tax Information and Planning Advice The Schmidt Tax Report (subscription site)

                                 https://www.schmidtreport.co.uk/

<u>Government Websites</u>

Health & Safety Executive   http://www.hse.gov.uk

Land registry   https://www.gov.uk/government/
organisations/land-registry

<u>Town Planning</u>

Planning Consultant   Town Planning Experts

                                 58 Northern Road

                                 Portsmouth

                                 PO6 3DT

023 9252 3352

http://www.tpexpert.org

Insurance

GSI Insurance

16 North Street

Rushden

Northamptonshire

NN10 6BU

01933 411888

http://www.gsiinsurance.co.uk

Land Search Tools

www.landinsight.io

http://www.rightmove.co.uk

https://www.zoopla.co.uk

http://www.uklandandfarms.co.uk

https://www.primelocation.com

https://www.onthemarket.com

https://www.gumtree.com

Miscellaneous

https://www.fiverr.com   (find designers

to create images for development or other marketing needs)

<u>Structural Warranty Provider</u> CRL (construction insurance specialists) https://c-r-l.com

A Note from Lloyd

Thank you for sparing the time to read this book. I hope you have gained some inspiration from it and it has motivated you to take your next steps, now that you have a better understanding of how to do so.

Regardless of what you choose to do going forward, please remember that whatever your dream or desire, nothing is too far out of reach if you approach it with dedication and persistence. If you're passionate enough about your dream, you can achieve it. Don't be someone who looks back with regret for never having tried.

My only regret is that I didn't start sooner. In fact, if you ask most successful business owners, I'm sure they would say the same.

But I did start. And that I have never regretted. We can't change the past. But we can change the future.

Contact me

If you have enjoyed reading this book please let me know – share your OSM moment(s) with me, let me know what part(s) of the book you liked best, and how it has helped you. And let me know how you get on with your challenge to send letters out to landowners. More importantly, share this book with people whom you think might benefit from it. The law of reciprocity may pay you kindly in return one day.

What lies ahead

Every year, things change. Lenders change their terms, their interest rates and fees. Legislation and planning fees change to meet the ever-shifting marketplace and economy. New lenders enter the market and old ones disappear. Governments change and new tax rules are legislated. It is critical to your success to keep up to date with the latest news.

To get the latest information, and updates on when future editions of this book are released, please visit us at www.whiteboxps.com/book.

Lloyd Girardi